Lacan and the Question of Consent

Clotilde Leguil explores the boundary between "consenting" and "yielding" from a Lacanian standpoint.

Starting from the definition Lacan gave to psychical and sexual trauma, this book makes the distinction between the ambiguity of consent and the experience of coercion. Clotilde Leguil refers to the *#MeToo* movement, campaigns against femicides and Vanessa Springora's book *Le Consentement* (Consent), elaborating on the various degrees of coercion to demonstrate that desire is not drive and that forcing leaves an indelible mark on the individual. Beyond the legal and contractual approach of consent, this book elaborates on the crucial stakes, both clinical and ethical, that this distinction entails.

Lacan and the Question of Consent will be of interest to psychoanalysts and psychoanalytic theorists. It will be relevant for academics and scholars of Lacanian studies, gender studies, feminism, and human rights.

Clotilde Leguil is a psychoanalyst and philosopher based in France.

Lacan and the Question of Consent

Why Yielding is Not Consenting

Clotilde Leguil

Translated by Domitille Krupka

Routledge
Taylor & Francis Group

LONDON AND NEW YORK

Designed cover image: Getty | ivan-96

First published in English 2026
by Routledge
4 Park Square, Milton Park, Abingdon, Oxon OX14 4RN

and by Routledge
605 Third Avenue, New York, NY 10158

Routledge is an imprint of the Taylor & Francis Group, an informa business

Céder n'est pas consentir. Une approche clinique et politique du consentement © Presses Universitaires de France/Humensis, 2021

British Library Cataloguing-in-Publication Data
A catalogue record for this book is available from the British Library

ISBN: 978-1-032-88265-9 (hbk)
ISBN: 978-1-032-88263-5 (pbk)
ISBN: 978-1-003-53695-6 (ebk)

DOI: 10.4324/9781003536956

Typeset in Times New Roman
by KnowledgeWorks Global Ltd.

To those who take the risk of saying,
To those who take the risk of writing.

Contents

By the Same Author

Je, Une traversée des identités, Puf, 2018.

L'Être et le genre, Homme/Femme après Lacan, Puf, 2015, réed. "Quadrige", 2018.

In Treatment, Lost in Therapy, PUF, 2013.

Sartre avec Lacan, *corrélation antinomique, liaisons dangereuses,* Paris, Navarrin Éditeur, "Le Champ freudien", 2012.

Les Amoureuses, voyage au bout de la féminité, Seuil, Paris, 2009.

Acknowledgements

For the English publication by Routledge:

The translation of my book "Céder n'est pas consentir" was made possible thanks to Domitille Krupka's committed and enthusiastic work, which has fulfilled her long-held desire.

I warmly thank my colleague from the New Lacanian School in Dublin, Florencia F. C Shanahan, for proofreading the translation with great rigour and generosity.

The publication of this translation by Routledge came into being by the trust placed in me by Susannah Frearson. Thank you to Carla Antonucci for her help on the index.

For the French publication by the Presses Universitaires de France:

Thanks to my publisher Monique Labrune, who first believed in this book from the start; she has always been attentive and in tune with my desire.

Thanks to Noémie Stephan for her diligence and invested proofreading and to Camille Auzéby for her support and enthusiasm.

Thanks to Laurent Dupont, president of the Ecole de la Cause Freudienne, for his receptiveness to my text "Céder n'est pas consentir" ("Boussole clinique", 14 July 2020, towards the 50th Journées de la Cause Freudienne on "Sexual Assault").

Thanks to David Halfon, the organizer of the Association of the Cause Freudienne Esterel Côte d'Azur on "sexual trauma" (Nice, 10 October 2020) who invited me to speak and engage with the members of the ACF on this delicate question.

Thanks to Bruno Durand for introducing me to the myth of Tereus and Philomela.

Thanks to Xavier who heard me and responded to my ideas during the development of this essay, allowing me to further elaborate my ideas.

Thanks to the joyful trio, Hector, Éléonore and Fleur, for their curiosity and genuine commitment to debating ideas.

Chapter 1

The "We" of Rebellion, the "I" of Consent

This essay, entitled *To Yield Is Not to Consent*, is in keeping with one of the political issues of the day: the globalization of the liberation of women's speech since 2017. The *#MeToo movement* is a landmark in the history of feminism, a watershed moment in a new liberation of women, through the social networks, the web, and the acceleration that goes with it.

This movement forces us to examine this unprecedented phenomenon and to try and analyse its effects.

Added to the *#MeToo* movement is the poster campaign against feminicide which resonates with the statement "to yield is not to consent": *Les Coleuses* (the gluers) pasted messages in black letters on white walls all over French cities. It was a visual statement of "no" which lent itself to be deciphered, like a message coming from elsewhere, denouncing that which could no longer be ignored. It was essentially a rebellion against the use of women's bodies for the sake of a jouissance which can go as far as abolishing a woman's life.

But this essay is also in keeping with the current publication of literary works which have given rise, for the first time ever, to an investigation in the first person of the question of consent in the fields of love and sexuality. It has led me, as a woman, a philosopher, and a psychoanalyst, to examine the motives of consent in one's existence.

If the rebellion of "We the women" expresses a collective "no," then whoever uses the singular "I" explores the ambiguity of a "yes." At the root of this essay is the encounter between what the walls of the city state, basically that there is a difference between "yielding" and "consenting" and a written account, *Consent,*[1] relating personal abuse which was not experienced as such at the time but only later, long after the facts occurred. Lastly, the publication of *La Familia Grande*[2] by Camille Kouchner will lead me to ask a final question: "in the name of what does the subject consent?" I will come back to it at the end of this essay. Albert Camus considered rebellion as an ultimate "no" which is also an assertion. "In other words, this 'no' affirms the existence of a borderline,"[3] he wrote at the start of his essay, *The Rebel*, in 1951.

It is the existence of this border between "to yield" and "to consent" which will be the focus of this essay. A frontier asserted in the "no" of the twenty-first century

DOI: 10.4324/9781003536956-1

women's rebellion, and which literature and psychoanalysis may explore, demonstrating its opacity.

Psychological Consequences of the #Metoo Movement

The political dimension which I will decipher finds its starting point in what we can call the beginning of a new era, the era of the liberation of women's speech through the #MeToo movement. This movement, which was followed by the striking and courageous testimonies of actresses, such as Adèle Haenel, has unveiled a hitherto silenced truth: the pervasiveness and magnitude of sexual harassment and abuse in the cinema industry, in the workplace, in politics, and elsewhere too. And this was happening everywhere. *All over the world.* This revelation, about the morals of some powerful people who had allowed themselves to satisfy their sexual desires, regardless of the desire of the other, spread overnight, after so many years, centuries even, of silence.

However, literature, here a first-person narrative, is also necessary and plunges us at the core of this distinction between "to yield" and "to consent." Literature introduces us to something else, to this intimate and mysterious realm of consent. Writing reacquaints the author with the subject. With writing, what is encountered is, to quote what Geneviève Fraisse also explains about consent, a measure of the truth of the subject.[4]

What I am interested in is the complexity of this undertaking, exploring the truth of the subject, and testifying to the truth of the trauma. This is the point on which the debate is focused, namely the status of speech for the subject who has had a bad encounter and bears witness to it not only in a legal context but more largely, to the other, an Other who is able to hear them.

It is therefore a question of positioning oneself between the "We" of rebellion and the "I "of consent. It is this double call which characterizes the current climate. Each one of us, male or female, positions themselves more willingly either on the side of the "we" or on the side of the "I." I said "climate," but I could have also said mood. Current times are characterized by anger and rebellion regarding what is made of women's bodies. But ours is also a time of liberation for another speech, through writing and literature, which tries to grasp what is unsayable in love, desire, and jouissance. Anger then is no longer the driving force; what has become the driving force is the necessity to explore trauma, its truth, and its opaqueness in order to recover from it.

This collective female movement, a new type of insurrection against harassment, new because it was borne by social media, by the virtual and viral world, was necessary to chart a new course that could lead to something else. As if there had been several logical times: first, the time of the collective "no," of the "we" also, with its power and strength; and secondly, the time of the "I," of the singularity of the trauma, when the unsayable effects of a bad sexual encounter and the ambiguity of consent were being examined. Without shame, since then blame had been placed back on the perpetrator.[5] This second period is crucial because it gives the "we" of rebellion another status. Here is my explanation.

The "We the women," at the centre of the political rebellion movement, immediately sparked off divisions between those who identified with the "We" of the *#MeToo* and others who did not see themselves in it, or not in this way, or who did not approve of the tone or the general condemnation "in general" of male domination and patriarchy. This "We" which emanated from a genuine desire to change the conditions in which women's bodies were treated, and to acknowledge their speech, may have deluded some into believing that utopia was possible. What they seemed to say was: "all of us have experienced the same things and all of us together can denounce the abuse; and the more we are the easier we will extricate ourselves from what was traumatic in our experience, in short, the more liberated we will be.

Now, it is also this communal sharing of trauma, a collective responsibility of the trauma which has limits. While it led to the recognition that women's bodies had been instrumentalized, it does not open onto a singular recognition of each woman's trauma. It is possible to shout "No," but the "No" must pave the way for each person's singular experience. Everything must be done so that the first "We" which was a legitimate "No" should not turn into a superegoic "We," the "we" of the authoritarian superego that would impose to each and every woman an identical version of their trauma – a common explanation and a uniform discourse on the causes and effects of the relationship between love and sexuality, on the powers of love and desire in the encounter with a partner or a pervert. In short, it is the mass support to a "We" – as if us women were all the same – which can backfire on the initial momentum of the rebellion.

This is where I wish to situate this essay. Starting from this "We" of the rebellion which has opened onto something else, in the direction of the "I" who speaks and writes and can say what rebellion alone cannot say. Rebellion is not concerned with details. It is also its strength. It is transmitted from one to the other and requires mass support. Yet, it is a detail that provides access to the truth and the real of trauma. I am going therefore to analyse this "we" of women's rebellion against sexual harassment, starting from the path which has been opened onto an intimate "I." Thanks to the "We" of the *#MeToo* movement which had preceded it, the "I" no longer needed to be hidden and ashamed of not knowing what it had consented or yielded to. It could now say, write, and be published.

The passage from the "We" to the "I" thus brought about effects which were to be felt beyond political recognition. Literature testifies to experiences of abuse, sexual harassment or rape told in the first-person narrative. It testifies to the necessity of finding a singular language to say what happened to the *me*. Literature moves us from the strength of the group and the power of digital technology which can transform common opinion, to the potency of the written word and the language of one woman only, to make the unspeakable element of trauma resonate, thereby touching an intimate point in each one. Therefore, it is also the poetry of words, the insurrectionary power of language, which makes it possible to indicate on which intimate point of the being's truth has the subject been struck by the sexual trauma and at which moment in their personal history the event took place, leaving an indelible scar.

What leads me to give my consent? What is this move originating in the most intimate part of the subject and in what is experienced in the body, which compels us to trust the desire of another to meet one's own desire and one's own being, through love and jouissance? It is this investigation into the impossibility to live a life without encountering this experience in which you open yourself to another, ultimately what consent means, which will be the subject of my essay. The necessity to recognize that psychological and sexual trauma is not rooted in consent but in the betrayal of consent will be posed.

Demonstrating the value of consent but also its ambiguous and at times enigmatic aspect for the subject who consents, such is my objective in this essay where I will delve into the opaque universe which a subject's consent constitutes.

Paradoxical Effects of Sexual Liberation

In January 2020, a much talked about book by Vanessa Springora entitled *Le Consentement*[6] [Consent] was published. It recounts in a unique way, an experience which plunges us, into the opaque world of consent. This account is that of Vanessa Springora who questions the "Yes" which led her to experience real sexual abuse. She relates the twists and turns of this consent and writes how a very young girl consented to a romantic relationship that was anything but love. This narrative forces us to ponder over this shift – made possible by the opaque nature of consent – a shift from desire to drive, from a love encounter to an experience of sexual abuse. In *Consent,* Vanessa Springora's aim is to explore, after the events took place, the web in which she found herself ensnared, from the initial desire and what she mistook for a romantic encounter, to the discovery that the trap had closed in on her.

Some encounters partake of the awakening of dreams. Circumstances are sometimes met for the subject to surrender its own self so well that they are totally unable to make a U-turn. Dreams have been awakened, the body has been involved, and nothing will ever be the same again. But in the bad encounter as is related in the book – at fifteen, the narrator fell prey to a 50-year old man using her for his own jouissance – the awakening experienced by the subject is rather of the order of a rupture, although she is unable to say it whilst the scenario is being played out. Writing about it thirty years later, the author tries to give an account of what happened, which has nothing to do with love anymore. But how is it possible to know this when it is the first time?

Reading *Consent* means being immersed in the "first time," immersed in the discovery of sexuality for a young girl, immersed in the consequences of a loss of virginity which was not consented to. This memoir, without any feeling of hate being ever expressed, is about a traumatic encounter and perversion. What is of interest to me is the mystery inherent in consent, what it can say about the concrete life of a subject, the mystery of consent, and its link with a form of feminine jouissance.

This memoir is finally about an epoch – the end of the 1970s and the 1980s – a time when everything seemed permitted and when sexual trauma was not always distinguished from the encounter and its mysteries. The book is also about an epoch during which a few intellectuals circulated petitions in favour of the liberation of men charged with child grooming, whilst shortly before then – amid the revolutionary wave of May 1968 – nobody started a petition in favour of a thirty-year-old woman, a teacher who was sentenced to jail and even banned from teaching because she was in love with one of her pupils. It is an epoch on which, a few years before the publication of Vanessa Springora's memoir, the writer Simon Liberati, in his 2015 book *Eva*, passed a very unfavourable judgement. This is a time, he wrote, when "the old deceitful attitude which is the hallmark of Sadean philosophy, advocates freedom to better subjugate the object of its concupiscence."[7] His essay is about Sade and his moral philosophy which is as cruel as the moral philosophy advocating renunciation of sexuality. In fact, if we are to believe Lacan in his text *Kant with Sade*, it is nothing but its reversal. The imperative of absolute enjoyment smoothens the way for the annihilation of the other's body.

The paradox is that this period born from the revolution of May 1968 and expanding from the 1970s to the 1990s almost is called a period of sexual liberation. What kind of sexual liberation is it exactly? How far can jouissance make progress without considering the presence of the other, and the desire of the man or the woman who becomes object? This is also what must be questioned, from the aphorism: "to yield is not to consent." What did this period want? It was a cheerful, creative, and emancipated period. It was a period made of novelty and of the rejection of the austere traditional authority, of the refusal of conformism, and the praise of imagination. It was envied in some respects, for its freedom and vitality, compared to our present times fraught with new norms. It is a period – the 1980s – which I, as a teenager, also experienced and loved.

What a striking contrast between the climate of the early twenty-first century, when the approach of the subject began to change little by little, becoming quantitative, more "neuro" than "psy," more objective than political too, and the climate of the 1970s and 1980s which bore the hallmark of excitement and freedom. Yet, afterwards, a question arises: Wasn't this period blinded by jouissance as by a new God? How are we to understand this call for jouissance, for sexual liberation which some will turn into an ideal of mastery of sexuality, without considering the partner, the other, more particularly women, but also children and teenagers? Forgetting to question the other's consent and desire disregards thereby the issue of femininity and the question of sexual awakening as an adventure which has nothing to do with education.

Everything seemed confusing then: the desire with the drive, the romantic encounter with sexual education, sexual emancipation with the freedom to abuse the other, and love transgression with incestuous crime. It seemed that in a few decades, "to yield" had become synonymous with "to consent," for the benefit of some who were fixated on jouissance without concern for the Other's desire and who thus instrumentalized consent. It was as if the claim to sexual freedom had produced a blind spot in the range of vision of the sexual relationships. Abuse was ignored and not even talked about, as if one person's desire justified abusing another, as if Freud's discovery of child sexuality meant that it was allowed to enjoy another's body, whatever their age or their ability to answer and to refuse.

Some wanted to forget at all costs that the "other's consent"[8] could be an obstacle to their right to jouissance, as François Regnault put it.

Consent also looks back at what happened at that time. The beauty of Vanessa Springora's memoir lies in her ability to plunge the reader into the darkness of consent for the subject who has consented. It is also to shed a personal light on this distinction between "to yield" and "to consent." Because what she consented to has nothing to do with what she had to yield to. She fully accepts responsibility for her contradictory behaviour as she asks herself: "how can one admit that one has been abused when one cannot deny one has consented [...] when one has felt desire?"[9] It is within this experience of betrayed consent that I wish to establish a distinction between "to yield" and "to consent." It is precisely because the subject has felt desire that he or she feels lost afterwards. So, what happened? What happened to her that led the emergence of desire turn into a nightmare?

Why did she wait so long, almost thirty years, before starting to write about this first time? New political conditions capable of welcoming this account favourably were necessary so that the risk taken by the writer should not turn back on her. A change of century was necessary. The *#MeToo* movement did pave the way for the possibility to greet this memoir. Admittedly, this movement, because of its scope, its planetary dimension, and its unheard-of scale, brought a major change. Vanessa Springora proved it herself. This movement was necessary to make the publication of her book possible. Yet, from a more intimate point of view, time was needed, a very long time was needed, for the devastating effects of her experience to be overcome and surmounted. What was needed too was an encounter with psychoanalysis and a few good encounters in her life for her to find again faith in speech, trust in desire, and the impetus to write.

To what extent did the *#MeToo* movement change the conditions of speech for women? I would argue that the expression "all together" made it possible to get out of a complex situation where trauma could be recognized only if it was proved. As if the general dimension of harassment was what was recognized through the *#MeToo* movement, before the question of the traumatic consequences due to a bad encounter for one woman only. Before exploring the effects of trauma, a spate of revelations had to be unleashed. "You are victims, and we believe you." Beyond the question of truth, it was about revealing the reality of a practice which thousands of women were confronted to.

If people believe you, then you can say what happened to you. Vanessa Springora was able from then on to write about this sexual abuse, starting with her own consent. It is with this word "consent" that she investigates the "yes" while her body said "no." This account is about a distorted pact, the betrayal of a consent given by a fifteen-year-old girl to a fifty-year-old man whom she considered a lover, her first lover, whilst he was in fact a predator. It deals with a moment of subjective disappearance and depersonalization.

Why psychoanalysis? Could speech do something about it? Yes, it could, because "consenting" and "yielding" are linked to the body and to speech. They are also linked to the unconscious and to the drive. A place is therefore needed to say what can't be said elsewhere, the retroactive effects of trauma, shame some-times, anxiety, inhibition, the marks left on the body, the subjective fracture which demands to be recognized in specific conditions of speech which cannot be public. There, social networks must be replaced by another space. Public speech cannot take responsibility for the singular effects of trauma. It is no longer possible to say "all together," since it is no longer a question of saying "no" but of saying "yes" to a plunge into the enigmatic traces left on the body by the trauma.

"To yield is not to consent" is a statement which can be deciphered, questioned, and scrutinized from the psychoanalytical approach to trauma. This is what I propose to show. There has often been a misuse of psychoanalysis at a time when sexual liberation may have been tempted to use Freud's discovery and Lacan's theory to legitimize all manifestations of the drive for the sake of a will to enjoy. Now, I want to show that psychoanalysis is precisely what makes it possible to draw an ethical distinction between desire and drive, between consent and forced consent, and between the meanders of love and sexual affairs and the abuse of the other's body. Taking up again the question of the delicate frontier between "to yield" and "to consent" to explore it further will lead me and us to a ground which is both clinical and political. For, before having been recognized as a matter of love concerning female subjects, consent was connected to the political field, to the social contract and the exit from the patriarchal power.

From the Political "We" to the "We" of the Love Pact

So, this essay will deal with the "We," the *we* of those who expressed themselves on the Web as they condemned the use of women's bodies without their consent. But it will also deal with another "We," that of the romantic encounter, the "We" of the encounter with a singular mode of speech, and the "We" of a turmoil in a body caused by the encounter with another body, which may be disarming. This "We" of the romantic encounter is not necessarily a reciprocal "We." It is certainly not a "We" of fusion between two people. In love, there is often asymmetry, discrepancy, misunderstanding and discord. But there is consent too. There is a "We" which transforms the being, when the experience is made of a real encounter. It is a "We" which allows the subject to dock in the Other's world, thanks to a particular speech which makes resonate what no other has ever told them. It is a "We" which makes up for the foreignness of the sexual drive.

So, my essay will be about the "I" who consents and gathers the marvelous effects of consent in their bodies. Because consenting is always a first-person sin-gular act. Consent is impossible for those who refuse to speak in their own names. Consent is both a withdrawal of the subject and a first-person act.

But I will also deal with what is shy of the "I," namely shy of the body which can experience a rupture when the other operates a forcing which is not consented to.

The absence of harmony in love and sexual relationships, expressed through Lacan's aphorism "There is no sexual relation," should not lead us to mis-recognize trauma. Saying that each one of us experiences the absence of sexual relation does not mean that forcing is the royal road to sexuality. There is no pre-established harmony between two beings whatever their gender, age, history, style, and background. This is understood. However, there can be forcing and rupture when one obeys the logic of the drive against the other's desire. This is what it is about.

If there is always a form of excess and transgression in jouissance, if the experience of jouissance obeys no rule, it does not imply that violence and coercion have something to do with a jouissance consented to by the other's body.

Love is what enables one individual's jouissance to consent to another individual's desire. The absence of love is what may give rise to a traumatic jouissance, when one human being yields to the other's demand without consenting to it. In this respect, jouissance is not the sign of love. The sign of love is situated elsewhere. If this elsewhere is missing, all that is left is an encounter with a jouissance which is demanding and imposed. An absolute jouissance causing terror, dread, shame, and disgust.

Twenty-first century women are right to rebel and shout. Thanks to the web, the "no" of women has reverberated beyond frontiers. "I rebel – therefore we exist,"[10] Camus wrote. Women who experienced sexual harassment found the means to turn their trauma into a political tool.

The "We are" in the form of the *#MeToo*" has been a means to find a place for the "no" of those who for too long had been deprived of speech.

Notes

1 Vanessa Springora, *Consent: A Memoir*, Transl. Natasha Lehrer, Harper Collins, 2021.
2 Camille Kouchner, *The Familia Grande, A Memoir*, Transl. Adriana Hunter, Other Press, 2022.
3 Albert Camus, *The Rebel: An Essay on Man in Revolt,* Transl. Anthony Bower, Vintage, 1992, p. 10.
4 Geneviève Fraisse, *Du consentement*, Paris, Seuil, 2017, p. 135.
5 See Sarah Abitbol's testimony, *Un si long silence*, Paris, Plon, 2020.
6 Springora, *Consent: A Memoir*.
7 Simon Liberati, *Eva*, Paris, Le Livre de poche, 2016, p. 165.
8 François Regnault, "Laissez-les grandir !", *La Cause du désir*, 2020, n° 105, p. 9.
9 Springora, *Consent: A Memoir*, p. 145.
10 Camus, *The Rebel*, p. 15.

Chapter 2

The Enigma of Consent

There is no enlightened consent. This is what makes the beauty of consent. Consent carries with it an element of enigma, of letting go, which is accompanied by a total ignorance of what one consents to, a destitution[1] even. Consent as the act of a subject is openness to the other, and the risk of letting the other cross the frontiers of its intimacy. In this respect, consent is always a leap into the unknown: without knowing, I trust the other's desire. Without knowing I believe in their words. Without knowing, I rely on their desire. This obscurity inherent in consent – this "yes" which is not based on knowledge but on a relation to desire – is also what gives it luster. It is because of this absence of transparency to oneself that consent acquires its value and reveals to me that I can say "yes" without being able to account for it rationally. It is from the mystery I can become for myself, when I experience desire that genuine consent occurs.

Obscure Consent

Consent is always frightening. Anxiety can emerge afterwards. Before too. It gives us cause for concern. Will this consent save me, or will it be my downfall? I don't know. But at the same time, I feel the irresistible character of consent as a choice full of life. It is because consent takes me by surprise that it is also a life force. My consent to the Other, to their speech, their body, and their desire, redefines my whole being as embraced, a body filled with emotion, a vital spark. A body which is both absorbed and revitalized by the Other. The giddiness of consent, this *cumsentire*, which tears me away from loneliness, also lies in the experience of destitution. I am defenseless; I do not belong to myself any longer. I am elsewhere. Other to myself. I do not feel so much in tune with the other as I do with my body now moved by the other. I say "yes" to the life manifesting itself in this body which is mine and yet seems foreign to me.

This takes place in a subdued tone. The one to whom I consent shares the enigma of this consent. They welcome it. They do not know why I say "yes" but they believe in this consent without it ever being of the order of a clear and rational act. So, the opacity of my consent can also be felt by the other as strange and confront them to this part of being which is always elusive in an amorous

DOI: 10.4324/9781003536956-2

encounter. The narrator of *The Captive*, by Marcel Proust, loves Albertine whom he is jealous of at the same time. He can see very well that her consent does not say everything about her. She is not "all" his for all that. The young woman he noticed on Balbec beach, among the gang of cheeky young women running over the beach, who even jumped over an old man's lying body, consents to love him. But what torments the narrator is that she eludes him despite her very consent. He thought that he would just have to meet her, and she would just have to say "yes," for him to possess her. But the "yes" did not put an end to the enigma Albertine represents for him.

The narrator experiences, through jealousy, the opacity of consent which does not reveal everything about Albertine's life, about her own desire, and her intimate life with others without him. Albertine's consent only serves to reinforce its elusive aspect. The narrator perceives that Albertine consents beyond him. He therefore unremittingly questions her about this mysterious life she has with others, female friends mostly, Andrée, Verteuil's daughter, and all those she does not mention to him. Her consent to desire and love for him does not cease on the frontier of their relationship. This is what he experiences when he is jealous, and this jealousy leads him to overplay his indifference towards her. He would like her to be captive of an exclusive consent by asking her to confess what she refuses to tell him. He loves the bird in her, which always escapes from its cage, "the marvelous bird of the first day"[2] while trying to make her the captive of his own world.

This is the enigma of consent in love and its effects.

The notion of "informed consent,"[3] invoked particularly in the field of medical practice, veils this opacity of consent which can be perceived in the field of love and sexuality. It diverts our attention from it. Where does the idea of "informed consent" originate from? In this formulation, the register of feeling, which is specific to consent, is overshadowed by the register of rationality. "Informed consent" means that consent stems from an act of reason. The illumination here comes from the enlightenments of reason as being the ability allowing me to know what I am saying and what I am doing. This notion of informed consent is contemporaneous with a medical practice in which paradoxically a form of distrust is present in the relationship between the doctor and the patient – where both doctor and patient are distrustful of each other. It is correlative to a demand of transparency which would reestablish the trust lost in the Other. Informed consent is demanded from the patient so that he or she should accept anything unpredictable that might happen, as is always the case with a medical act, and so that this unpredictable element should not be concealed from them by the doctor. It is demanded as a form of protection and guarantee. It is also correlative to a due, to the doctor's duty to inform him and not to treat him without reporting on what he decides to do to cure him. It is the doctor's word which is supposed to be transparent and not to veil the medical conditions, but it is also the patient's agreement which is supposed to be given with full knowledge of the facts. "Informed consent" means that the patient is fully aware of the risks he exposes himself to, aware of the unpredictability of some reactions of the body to a medical and surgical intervention. "Informed consent" means that the patient has been warned and that he has accepted the risk. It means that he has been told about it beforehand and that, somehow, he knows with complete transparency the risk he runs.

But, in fact, the patient consents without knowing.

The adjective "informed," "enlightened," leads one to believe that there is a rational foundation of consent. However, this adjective which also evokes the light cast on consent tends to veil the obscure origin of this "*cum-sentire,*" which means "to feel at ease with someone, to trust them." Consent is closely related to the encounter with an Other and to the effect this encounter can produce on me. "Consent, whether explicit or implicit, assumed or expressed, is always an act which has to do with a subject's intimacy,"[4] as Geneviève Fraisse puts it. This adjective, which appeals to the Enlightenment and to each person's responsibility, qualifies the term consent, so that it should become an act of reason. But isn't it precisely to divert attention from the fact that there is no rational foundation of consent, that we absolutely want it to be "informed"? Isn't it to obliterate the fact that consent has its reasons which reason knows nothing of? This absence of rational foundation to my act, this absolute choice to consent without any justification, can arouse fear.

The patient's informed consent is therefore required in medical practice so that the assumed trust should be made explicit. I must accept the contingency of what may happen – for the doctor to be also protected in case something does happen – so that I should not legally turn against him and argue that I did not know. In fact, I did not know, and I can't know. This "yes" is based, not on the assertion "I knew the risk I was running" but on the trust in the doctor's knowledge and ethics. This "yes" never means "I knew" but "I recognize you." "To you I can say 'yes' because I believe in your authority." Even though I do not know, I must say "yes." This opacity of consent, visible in the field of love, is also present in the field of care. One could even go as far as saying that consent in love tells the truth about any form of consent. It is precisely because I do not know what the exact consequences of a medical act will be that my consent is required. I must say "yes" without knowing. If I wait until I know, I always say "no." I keep postponing my "yes." I wait a little longer until I am sure before I say "yes." Yet I am never sure. I can never be sure as far as knowledge is concerned. I can only be sure as far as desire is concerned.

I say "yes," even though I don't exactly know what I consent to and that's how it is.

The Risk of Consent

Consent is not of the order of knowledge; it is of the order of a faith in the encounter with another who knows something I don't know. He can enlighten me if he wishes to, about his decisions, his acts, his choices; but he can't, for all that, make his knowledge clear to the point of rendering it accessible to me. I only know it is "yes" because I have faith in him. With consent I tie myself to him. Consent appeals more to belief than to reason. Thus, with consent, there is always a possibility to be mistaken, to say "yes" to a love relationship, and, in the end, to find oneself trapped in another story which one has not chosen. In consent, there is a feeling of absolute risk which is also a game with one's own life. In every consent, there is a wager. I stake everything. I consent to lose. Accordingly, consent in love affairs and desire reveals the truth of consent which is at work in every other field. Consent in love is an intimate act which I alone can do, which nobody else can do in my place and which transforms me. There too, it is impossible for me to be enlightened by the other's lights. The others, those close to me, those less close, can never know in my place if I was right to consent. They can judge if they want to. They can believe that they know better than me what is good for me. But I alone can give my consent. I cannot entrust anyone with the power to consent in my place. So, in that sense, I am responsible for the consent I have given. I am responsible for what happens to me once I have consented. But up to what point?

In a sexual and love relationship, I give my consent knowing, or at least believing I know, who I consent to, but without knowing why. This responsibility is not based on mastery but on a desire. I experience my desire as an act which has committed me elsewhere, an act which has displaced and embarked me to a place where I accepted to lose something in order to discover something else. A place I had no knowledge of. Where can this act lead me? Will I be able to backtrack? Consent is an irrevocable act.

Once I have given my consent, how can I take it back if my consent has been betrayed? Is it possible to take it back? Take what back? How can I recover what I have lost in my consent? When there is a misdeal between what a subject consented to and what he encountered, a dangerous abyss opens below him. Is he responsible for this misunderstanding? It is impossible to spend one's existence without ever consenting to anything. Refusing to consent is not only refusing something to someone, but often it is also refusing something to yourself. Consent confronts me with a wager on my life from a relation to the Other. It is also a wager on my body for "there is no consent without body."[5] Consent has its pleasures too and shows the way to a new continent in which I apprehend another subject in myself when the person met lives up to my consent. I cannot spend my life saying "no." But I can choose to whom I say "yes." I can choose the moment when I let consent take care of the situation and move me elsewhere.

Ambiguity of Feminine Consent

Is consent a typically feminine act in respect to love and sexuality? What is certain is that taking a woman's consent into account marks a turning-point in the history of consent. We will see that. But beyond that, there may also exist a subtle and secret connection between consent and femininity and even consent "to" femininity, provided femininity is regarded as something different from a norm or a natural condition. Consent may reveal something of femininity as a bodily experience of jouissance. Consent may reveal how much the body matters. Consent may be intensified on the feminine side, if we are to believe Freud and Lacan, for whom "becoming a woman" has nothing to do with a social or natural programme or an obligation but rather with a consent based on an encounter. Consent on the feminine side would be consent to another, but also consent to the other in oneself, consent to the strangeness of femininity as an unclear experience. Such is the ambiguity of feminine consent which exposes the relation to desire and answers the demand of the other which can sometimes be opaque. All these dimensions of being are summoned up by the event which consent constitutes. The awakening desire, the relation to what the other wants, the enigma of what he expects of me, and of what I am ready to give in order to know. What does the one to whom I consent exactly want from me? Do they really love me? Can they lose me? Consent always implies crossing a frontier, taking a step towards the other, moving one's body and putting it at stake while at the same time experiencing anxiety on the borders of the territory of desire. The fear of taking the plunge a little too hastily mingled with an intensified feeling of life because one has thrown oneself into it. The risk taken to let go of oneself in order to knot one's destiny to another's. Is it because consent is always ambiguous that it is inauthentic? Is this ambiguity a sign of duplicity, distortion, untruth? No, it is not. To bear the ambiguity of consent is to accept that its value lies in the fact that it is not enlightened, informed. It is both a "yes" and an "I don't know." It is accepting the difficulty to know what consent implies, as a difficulty which carries a truth about desire. Hence, the double betrayal of whomever takes advantage of consent which means consenting to trust someone without knowing what the other's intentions are. Being able to bear the opaqueness of consent can sometimes even mean not to recoil before the enigma that the other's desire is for me – and which I cannot rationally understand. Ambiguity does not deprive consent from authenticity, it adds complexity to it. Consent, just like the relation to desire and jouissance, involves my body as a sexuated being. It involves this body in which things happen which I do not understand and yet feel. Things which are me and not me, things which I see coming back, and which, at times, dispossess me of myself. Affects, turmoil, emotions.

In this sense, consent is always consent to the body as foreign to oneself. Becoming oversensitive to the other's response, the consenting subject is filled with wonder at the discovery that he is transformed. "*Cum-sentire.*" So, the beauty of consent, its dazzling splendour should be defended. Consent is the other side of rejection of the other, distrust and non-recognition. However, it must be clearly distinguished from another experience which refers to another obscurity: that of sexual and psychological trauma.

Notes

1 The word *dénuement* is translated throughout the book as "destitution," and is to be distinguished from *destitution* as it appears in Chapter 4.
2 Marcel Proust, *Albertine Gone,* Transl. Terence Kilmartin, Chatto & Windus; First English Edition, 1989.
3 In French "consentement éclairé," literally "enlightened consent." [TN]
4 Geneviève Fraisse, *Du Consentement*, Seuil, Paris, 2017, p. 24.
5 Fraisse, *Du Consentement*, p. 127.

Chapter 3

The Frontier Between "to Yield" and "to Consent"

The enigma of consent, in the field of love and sexuality, can therefore only be deciphered if we take the aphorism "to yield is not to consent" seriously. It is necessary to establish a distinction between what has to do with consent, its ambiguity, its beauty, and what has to do with encountering a forcing in the body. "To yield is not to consent," it is true, and yet "to yield" and "to consent" are very close in the French language. It is this frontier that I am exploring, the necessity of this frontier. The abolition of the frontier between "to yield" and "to consent" leads to a danger. The danger of not recognizing the sexual trauma or even the psychological trauma anymore; the danger of no longer having the means to distinguish between a "yes" – even a discreet, reserved, modest, unconfessed, secret yes – and what has to do with an act of violence exerted on another person.

The Ethical Necessity of a Distinction

"Yielding" is connected to trauma. Trauma doesn't originate in consent although it may put it at stake, handle it, use it, and extort it. The subject who is being forced, very often no longer knows if he has consented or not. He may have said "yes" to something at the beginning without being able to say "no" to what happened afterwards, being committed as he was to this first "yes." "Am I in some way responsible for what happened to me?" This is the question that a subject who has had a bad encounter always asks himself. Did he unknowingly consent to what happened to him? Shouldn't he have said "no" more clearly, shouted "no" even and run away quickly? Didn't I let it all happen, although I could have defended myself? As a result, am I not also to blame? I am ashamed and this shame is covered by the impossibility to talk about it, as though I had to conceal this trauma which suddenly emerged. It is this jouissance without the other's mediation which has traced in my body the way towards a jouissance that I did not want, giving rise to shame. Perversion knows how to manipulate the ambiguity of consent, which always makes desire unclear and unsettling for the subject himself. It knows how to produce in the other's body this effraction that petrifies the subject. It knows how to cover the ambiguity of desire with the obscenity of the drive in all its nudity. The sexual trauma, a psychological and bodily trauma, can stem from a betrayal of

DOI: 10.4324/9781003536956-3

consent. Thus, it takes a traumatized subject back to the enigma of his own consent. Without fail.

Yet, "to yield is not to consent."

This distinction sheds an ethical light on the question of consent and trauma in regard to sexual and love life, but perhaps also in regard to the relation to the Other in general, in the field of politics.

Because "yielding," in the way I analyse it, from an approach which is both clinical and political, not only concerns sexuality and love but also life in society, professional life, and the life of our historical conditions. In the field of work and of professional life, there are also traumatic experiences. For here too, the subject has consented to a certain commitment on the basis of a work contract, and he suddenly finds himself trapped in something altogether different, in a form of alienation which can arouse anguish. "To yield without consent" in the work- place is no longer being able to answer to what is demanded, asked, extorted, in any other way than by carrying on all the same, despite everything. It means not knowing any longer if one must trust what one feels, this unease, this form of nausea verging sometimes on panic. "To yield" is then to feel that not only do you work for the Other but against yourself. It is no longer "feeling with the other," but "feeling one works against oneself," against the consent one had given at the start. It is feeling that a border has been crossed by the other and we can no longer pull ourselves together, convinced as we are that what we believe we must invest in our job is never enough. It never stops, it is never enough, I could have always given more and done better. The contract is not a guarantee. It is not sufficient to protect me from this moment when I can feel overwhelmed by what is required of me as if by a categorical imperative. As Deleuze showed, the contract can also be the tool of a sadomasochistic relationship in which one enjoys humiliating the other, on the basis of what was agreed at the beginning. Thus, "Things must be said, promised, announced, carefully described before being carried out."[1] The contract, which can be a tacit agreement, is also what establishes a form of silence. From the moment you have signed, I will no longer address you, I will no longer speak to you, you will carry out what you must carry out because you should know what you must do without even my telling you. Violence rests on silence. He who has consented is no longer spoken to or listened to. He is encouraged to carry out his job and give more and more of himself until he is deprived of his vital force. Since the advent of digital relationships, the condi- tions for the exercise of such power over people are being made easier: writing e-mails which the other does not understand, failing to answer when he asks for explanations, and finally letting him be plagued by his torments until he sub- mits to this silence as if to an authoritarian presence which never lets go of him. The body can then sound the alarm bell: I can no longer sleep, I am exhausted to the point that I no longer feel present with anyone, I no longer "feel with" but "without" as if my consent had turned against my desire. I am eaten away by all the tasks I have to carry out, by what the Other wants from me without saying it. And yet I carry on working, even more, as if it were a categorical imperative which it had become impossible for me to avoid. I must make it through, I must get by. I can't fall apart.

One day it is too late to make a U-turn: burnout.

One can speak of the "masochism" of the person who lets things happen to him, but isn't it rather anxiety that comes from not knowing, at times, how far one must go to obtain a form of recognition from the other? An anxiety that leads you to let it happen by putting your body to the test? The argument of masochism must not lead us to ignore the betrayal of the person who forces or abuses consent. Masochism, namely this inclination to make oneself suffer, is also an indication that the subject meets with a situation in which he can't get his bearings anymore and from which he must extract himself. The subject's consent can be instrumentalized in a romantic encounter, as well as in the family or professional world. There can be consent to love and in the end, an encounter with something which was not love but sexual abuse wearing the mask of love in order to operate. There may be consent to silence out of a belief in an authority. There may also be, in the professional world, a desire to do "well," even to do "everything" for a job, a boss, a manager, in the name of an ideal or an ideology. When this desire to "do well" encounters the other's authoritarian or perverse attitude, it can condemn the subject to obey beyond what he has consented to. What emerges then, to quote Frédéric Gros, is "over-obedience."[2] This modality of obedience is a form of submissiveness to what I do not want. It is because I "force" myself to obey that I feel myself at the same time guilty of not obeying enough. This is the very principle of what Freud and Lacan called the Superego. The more I force myself, the more guilty I am of obeying without really meaning to but because I force myself to. The more I mistreat myself, the more demanding is the Superego, expecting me to obey better. This is where the demands of the other meet the inner demand of the subject. Being overly obedient is not only obeying the other but obeying the inner order coming from the moral authority of the Superego. When the subject obeys beyond what he assumes is expected of him in order to prove that he is utterly devoted to his task, to prove that what he is expected to do and what he accomplishes is one and the same thing, to prove that he gives all his time and energy to what is becoming the only goal in his existence, this is when the border between "to yield" and "to consent" has been crossed. That is to say, when you don't allow yourself to think any longer, to trust what you feel, to listen to the signals of the body which express a silent malaise, anxiety, or sometimes disgust, when you obey and try to do always better. Being overly obedient is being poles apart from one's desire. It is already the sign of what the subject has yielded to, namely the sign of anxiety. If you go on trampling on your desire, if you go on overly obeying something else, one day it all breaks down and you find yourself in the dark, wondering where you are.

A Frontier at the Level of the Body

"To yield" has nothing to do with "yes" and "no," with the perspective of the satisfaction of desire sometimes postponed, with the ambiguity and the dialectics of the "I want to" and "I don't want to," "I want to but not immediately," "I don't want right now," "I might want to later." "To yield" in the sense of trauma or overly obeying is not consenting. "Yielding" is both to endure forcing and to force oneself. This is also where the mystery of trauma lies. Not only may there be bad encounters with the other, but there are bad encounters with oneself too, with this strange life partner which is my body, with what Freud and Lacan called the Super-ego, located at the point where language and body meet. This is how complex the notion of "yielding" is. I will show it. "Letting it happen"[3] has different degrees to it; it can go as far as "forcing" oneself, beyond what the body can bear.

Writing about this frontier implies facing the obscurity of consent, the enigma of one's own consent, and the subjective disappearance caused by trauma.

Let's come back to love and to sexual life. I argued that there was a closeness between "yield" and "consent." Yet, the contiguity between the two terms doesn't mean that one word can be confused with the other. A frontier does exist between the two. It is here that the distinction becomes necessary for reasons which are both ethical and clinical. It is precisely because from the outside, from a sheer behavioral point of view, "to yield" can resemble "to consent," even be confused with it, that it is necessary to have a clinical approach to consent and affirm the radical difference between "yielding" and "consenting." How is it possible to distinguish a subject who "yields" from a subject who "consents"? How can we know? Can this distinction be proved? Is it possible to prove that there has been a trauma? When consent is postponed, put off, adjourned, doesn't it eventually occur because the subject stops refusing, because the subject yields something? In that case, "consenting" would resemble "yielding."

So why should we differentiate between "yield" and "consent" if "consenting" implies "yielding"? Consent can pave the way for "yielding." This is the risk. But it doesn't mean in the least that "to yield" and "to consent" are the same thing. Who can tell if there has been consent between two human beings? Only the words of the subject concerned can reveal this frontier. Consent introduces us to the question of enunciation. "I consent." Nobody but the subject himself can say if he has yielded or consented. There is here something which nobody can do in the subject's place. He alone can say: "I consent." Because the frontier is situated in the subject's body. Whoever claims he can speak in the subject's place is already in a position of control. As if he knew what the subject himself does not know. As if he controlled what happened in the other's body and knew what was for him pleasure and what was displeasure. "Yielding" or "consenting" appeals to testimonies. The subject concerned must say himself. But sometimes, the subject does not even know – or rather he no longer knows. He questions himself about his consent because something happened in his body which he did not necessarily approve of, but which has become part of him now. "Beyond the pleasure principle," Freud said. No longer agreeing with the remaining marks of the sexual trauma, commemorations of this trauma, traces which will never be erased, also means not to agree with one's body anymore. It is a way to say "no" to oneself when the "no" declared to the other had no effect or could not be said. It is then the body which testifies to the truth of what happened for a subject. From his body, marked by the experience of an encounter which has left painful and unreadable hieroglyphs, the traces of the traumatic event, the subject can try to read the enigma of the trauma. What happened? What remains for me, of this traumatic event?

Does Silence Mean Consent?

The saying "silence is consent" pertains to this omission of the distinction between "yield" and "consent." It even pertains to this obliviousness. One must, therefore, against this common preconception, state the following aphorism: "Silence does not mean consent."

Silence can have different meanings. Admittedly, it can refer to consent kept secret. There can be some jouissance in remaining silent and in this case, silence means "yes." But the saying "Silence means consent" universalizes a possible and particular meaning of the term silence, by overstepping the desire of the person who is silent and by inevitably interpreting it as a "yes." "To keep quiet" has two meanings; it either means "to refuse to say" or "not to be able to say anything." This is the whole difference between: "not wanting to say that I want to," out of modesty, strategy and a taste for mystery, and "not being able to say that I do not want to," out of apprehension, fear, dread. Before saying "Silence means consent," one should consider the effect of stupefaction produced by the act of forcing: trauma cuts off all access to speech. This is actually its distinctive feature. Afterwards, what caused trauma remains outside the realm of speech, rejected from the history to which I have access, fixed elsewhere, present in the body but not put into words. Not worn away by time, the effect of trauma, like a foreign body deeply embedded in the flesh, continues to act in it as on the first day. It does not erode. This is how Freud first defined the effect of psychological trauma.

So, the question is no longer: "does silence mean consent or not?" but "how can trauma be eventually put into word given that it cannot, by definition, be symbolized"? Whoever was unable to utter a word whilst something was taking place in their body which they disapproved of, will they find the means, one day, to say something to someone? Will they find the means within themselves, and will they find the means with the other? Psychological trauma concerns the body. Speaking about what happened in the body when something has been "ceded" is a new risk to take.

Will he be heard by another or will his words only be met with rejection?

"What causes trauma cannot be spoken." It cannot be said, not only out of modesty or restraint, but because the effect of trauma hits the body in such a way that language is somehow short-circuited. As a result, the subject who has suffered from trauma has his lips sealed. "Whoever is silent does not speak because he can no longer say anything." "Whoever is silent" has become speechless. "Whoever is silent" is condemned to silence because what has broken into his body can't be put into words. It has no name. Language has not provided any word to say it. Impossible to say.

So how can trauma be recognized? The paradox of trauma is that "he who is silent" sometimes comes back to the scene where the trauma occurred. Hence the misconception of "retroactive" consent. Hence, this dangerous idea: "If he goes back, it means that he wanted to, that he liked it, that he consented." Yet, this return, this repetition of the trauma does not mean consent. It should not mean that. On the contrary, it means a nightmare. It will be difficult albeit necessary to demonstrate this point. The fact that the subject feels trapped in the repetition of his own trauma, that he goes back to it and can't free himself from it, does not signify that he consents. It is also here that the clinical approach makes it possible to get a clearer idea of what is at play. Freud identified this mysterious phenomenon which he called the repetition of the drive. This return, this "repetition compulsion," does not stem at all from the subject's will. Another logic is at work, the logic of the drive which encourages the subject to seek satisfaction at the risk of being detrimental to the life of the human being himself. It is this logic of the death drive which accounts for the recurrence of traumatic experiences.

Trauma is absolute loss. The subject returns to it because he does not know what he has lost in the traumatic experience. He doesn't have the words, but his body knows. He returns to it to find out how he can recover what has been torn away from him. He returns to it to try and catch up with his lost body. Trauma is this experience in which you lose your body. I have lost my body.

Notes

1 Gilles Deleuze, *Présentation de Sacher-Masoch*, Paris, Minuit, 1967, p. 18. *Masochism: Coldness and Cruelty,* 1989.
2 Frédéric Gros, *Disobey! A Philosophy of Resistance*, Transl. David Fernbach, Verso Books, 2020, p. 99.
3 In French "*se laisser faire.*"

Chapter 4

Consent

Intimate and Political

What gives consent its value as a notion is that it is at the junction of two fields, the intimate and the political. Consent as the experience of the subject who gives his consent is part of the concrete and sometimes secret life of each one. It may be consent in but also consent to what is asked or desired by another person in particular. Consent is what ties me to a commitment or a word I have said. And this occurs against a backdrop of enigma for, as I have explored since the beginning of my essay, the subject does not know why he said "yes" but feels he is tied to this "yes" in which he believes. Consent thus binds me to time. I said "yes" to a future. I said "yes" to a time I do not know yet but to which I have accepted to commit. On the basis of this consent, I may find myself caught in an adventure I had not expected and whose springs I was completely ignorant of at the moment when I said "yes," but from which, as of now, I can no longer extract myself. It follows that consent can lead to a "yielding," that is to say, a trauma.

If I now consider the political field, is this also the case? I realize that here too, consent is the place of an ambiguity. It can pave the way for an unexpected experience of forcing, an experience which, surprisingly enough, rests upon my consent.

Let's go back a little. Consent acquired a particular value in political philosophy from the eighteenth century onwards, among the theoreticians of the social contract, when it came precisely to distinguishing force from right. It was the theoreticians of the social contract of the seventeenth and eighteenth centuries, Hugo Grotius, Thomas Hobbes, and Jean-Jacques Rousseau, who placed the notion of consent at the core of the relationship between the citizen and society. Thus, at the root of civil law is "the obligation one imposed upon oneself through one's own consent."[1]

This is the very meaning of the "social pact" which is at the basis of the social state. Even if I never actually signed any pact before entering society, legally speaking, it is as if I had done so. It is this tacit pact which is the foundation of my duties as well as of my rights. Consent is hence a new modality of obedience. To obey is no longer to comply with the other's order or demand, it is to choose to abide by an authority one recognizes as legitimate. It is to submit to a law the moment one has consented to recognize this law as just. If I don't obey anymore, somehow, I am betraying myself and my own commitment.

DOI: 10.4324/9781003536956-4

Against the Right of the Strongest, the Consent of the Subject

So, this is a change of paradigm that concerns the source of authority. It is no longer the Other -God, the lord, the master, the King – who consents to grant me the right to live, and who can decide that I must die, it is I who, as a subject, consents to abide by the authority I recognize as just. The change in meaning of the term consent makes it possible to waive one's natural right and accept to submit to what Thomas Hobbes calls "the sovereign" and Jean-Jacques Rousseau the "general will." To quote Frédéric Gros: "consent is regarded as the rational kernel of obedience to the laws of the city."[2]

Nobody can oblige me to obey an illegitimate authority which would only impose itself by force. Authority doesn't stem from nature. Its value is established by laws alone, which state that it has been chosen by the people who recognizes it as just. In *The Social Contract* of 1762, Rousseau thus criticizes the notion of right applied to slavery, as a contradiction in terms. Right cannot be grounded on a power relation. Slaves are those who had to yield to force, not those who recognize a lawful authority. They are subjected to alienation in accordance with an unfair domination. Consequently, they don't have to obey an illegitimate authority. No force can invoke right to exert its hold over individuals. "Let us then admit that force does not create right and that we are obliged to obey only legitimate powers."[3] The right of the strongest is not a right but a power relation.

This distinction between right and force is fundamental to think the idea of legitimate authority. The notion of consent which lies at the origin of the political power, equates to an exclusion of force. To say this in more psychoanalytical terms, it is a question of excluding forcing from the political field and thinking a social bond which is based on consent and not on trauma. Pascal's verdict according to which "Having been unable to strengthen justice, we have justified might," is turned upside down. Justice must be strong and therefore all authority which is only based on force must be made illegitimate. Thus, the pact commits each subject: I have signed with society a contract that cannot be undone. I have consented to enter society provided society itself guarantees security, freedom, and justice.

It is because of a tacit consent that each citizen obeys the Sovereign whom he recognizes as embodying the general will. Living in society means respecting this social contract which makes it possible for each citizen to respect his duties and his rights. It is because the law embodies the general will, which is not the will of everybody, but the general will in each one, that one should submit to it. The "will" which is expressed by the general will does not concern people's own personal interests but the common good. If people obey, it is in accordance with each person's consent to "want" not only his own good and his particular interest, but the general interest and the collective good. In brief, the cause of the general will must triumph over the cause of the individual will.

Within the social contract, consent is "obedience to a law which we prescribe to ourselves."[4] It is therefore a new form of obedience, not founded on nature or tradition but on an act of reason. This obedience is at the same time a recognition of my capacity to choose what I obey. Thus, at the end of the *Social Contract*, Rousseau writes: "There is but one law which, from its nature, needs unanimous consent. This is the social pact."[5] The other laws do not necessarily require unanimity to be enforced; the social pact, however, is the inaugural law none can violate. On that point, the compliance of all is required.

The notion of social pact also introduces an act from the subject at the source of obedience. It changes thereby the meaning of consent which up to then, did not refer to the consent from "the subject" but to the consent expected, hoped for, asked by the subject from an Other, under whose authority he placed himself, whether it be the father's or the king's consent. The notion of pact summons up a subjective compliance from the subject, contrary to the submission to the strongest which is sheer yielding.

If society must be built on Law and if only an authority built on Law can require obedience, it follows that society, by virtue of this inaugural contract, rules out the right of the strongest. Thus, it is no longer on account of a natural and divine power that the King reigns, but owing to the consent of his subjects to whom he owes security and part of his freedom. The authority of a King over his subjects is legitimate only if it is chosen by those who submit to it. It is an established authority worth something only if it is considered as such. In short, with Rousseau, to be born free is also to remain free in society. It means submitting only to the authority one recognizes. Submitting to laws and not to a master.

Fathers Deposed

To base power on the citizens' consent is also to reject the analogy between political power and family power. The sovereign's authority is not identical to the authority of the father over his children. If political power is based on the social contract and if it is only a transfer of each citizen's will to the sovereign who embodies the general will, it is then no longer conceived with reference to the power of the father over his children. The paternal power is no longer the model of political authority, nor is it the model of justice. The power of the monarch over his subjects has nothing in common with the natural power of a father over his children. The paternalist conception of power is thus challenged by the theoreticians of the social contract. Subjects are not children but human beings who are free and equal in rights. In short, subjects must also abandon the idea that they are protected by the political power as they would be by a father.

Not only is the power of the father no longer the model of political power but it also becomes transformed by political power. What a father, as the lawful holder of authority is, only depends on nature as long as the children need the father to survive. "Yet the children remain attached to the father only so long as they need him for their preservation. As soon as this need ceases the natural bond is dissolved. [...] If they remain united, they continue so no longer naturally, but voluntarily; and the family itself is then maintained only by convention."[6] Thus, Rousseau argues that, once sons and daughters are no longer children, the bond with the father becomes dependent on consent.

In the eighteenth century, consent moves on the side of the "I," while it had been on the side of the Other. It is no longer a permission but a free and responsible choice to submit to a power recognised as just. It follows then that the social contract overturns the founding principle of authority. Authority does not come from the Other anymore but from the subject who consents to it. Each exercise of authority derives its legitimacy from the citizens' inaugural consent. Tacitly, each citizen must say "yes" to what is the general will, for this will is his as a citizen capable of aiming at the common good before his own. The pact involves the citizen's commitment, his initial "yes." To sum up, obedience must be founded on justice and not on strength. But is this "yes" an act of reason only?

The term "social pact" – which gives its title to chapter six of the *Social Contract*, where Rousseau defines the essence of this pact which leads human beings to forgo their natural freedom and substitute it for a civil liberty – adds a supplementary dimension to that of contract. The question is to know whether this supplementary dimension does not take us away from the purely rational field.

The pact is not quite identical to the contract. It is much more than a mere contract. It is a commitment towards another which rests on a faith in the other's words, a faith which may be linked to love, admiration, or recognition, but which cannot be wholly expressed in rational terms. Inherent in the pact is a form of devolution to a speech in which you believe. In the pact, there is an act, which is no more based on reason but on desire. The subject therefore entrusts himself to a will (the general will) from a consent to trust this mode of government without being afterwards able to extract himself from it. The social pact ties the subject not only to the others and to the laws but to his own consent.

Forced Political Consent

We may ask if founding the exercise of power on the pact and on consent guards against forcing. In other words, can consent be extorted? As he is defining obedience as the act of obeying freely to the general will, Rousseau adds this mysterious precision: "In order then that the social pact may not be an empty formula, it tacitly includes the undertaking, which alone can give force to the rest, that whoever refuses to obey the general will, shall be compelled to do so by the whole body. This means nothing less than that he will be *forced* to be free."[7] The use of force resurfaces here as no longer originating in nature but in the whole body politic, now in possession of the consent which made it sovereign in the first place. What is happening here? It becomes impossible to disobey. "Consent makes it impossible to unlock obedience."[8]

If the theory of the social contract shows progress in the order of justice concerning sovereignty and its origin, it does not guard against a power relation nor does it protect the subject from being crushed. This is what history will demonstrate. Consent becomes a kind of imperative which commits me in the future while at the same time removing the right of withdrawal from me.

Once this consent – that of the citizen considered as a subject- is placed at the root of power, it is also this consent which can be extracted and demanded by a power which cannot be legitimized without it. The possibility, always looming, of instrumentalizing consent then arises. If the paradigm of obedience has changed, the power which will be exercised, including through force, will not be limited to submission, it will require consent to submission. The obedience demanded by an authoritarian power which pretends to be just is situated beyond behavioral obedience. It is a question of giving the impression that the population is consenting while in truth the exercise of terror prevails. What is demanded is, to use the words of Frédéric Gros again, of the order of an "over-obedience": an obedience which demonstrates, beyond submission, consent to this submission. An obedience which displays the signs of a subject's choice and support to erase the marks of fear and submission. Doesn't it mean then, that a shift towards the Sadean pact is taking place? The victims of a regime which terrorizes them must, in addition, legitimize this power by giving it their consent.

In this respect, consent is distorted. The aim is to extort consent, in truth to obtain the subject's total submission, his complete subjection, that of his body but also that of his thoughts and even his dreams. The "We" the subject submits to has nothing to do anymore with the "We" which expresses a desire to build a community, the "We" of a common cause or of a general will present in each. It is the "We" of the authoritarian superego that replaces the first "We." The subject is then crushed by a "We" that requires his consent. This is also the meaning Lacan gave to a form of revolutionary demand when he spoke of a *revolutionary superego*. Before him, Camus investigated the distinction between rebellion and revolution. The distinction between "to consent" and "to yield" bears similarity to the difference between rebellion as an inaugural act which says "no" to the Other in accordance with the assertion of a desire, and revolution which, if we are to believe Albert Camus, is not always faithful to the initial impetus of the rebellion. Consent, which is assertion and choice, acceptation, and recognition, then turns against the subject himself and finally becomes submission and resignation. To consent then means "yielding." The psychological harassment exerted by a totalitarian regime aims at obtaining through force the consent which the subject refuses to give. It aims at depriving him of his own ability to consent. The "I consent" of the pact becomes a submission to a "you must consent" of dictatorship. "Consent [acquiescence] to humiliation, that is the true characteristic of twentieth-century revolutionaries,"[9] Camus wrote about individual terrorism.

Winston thought he could deceive power by disobeying only in his thoughts, his dreams, and even his nightmares. He was obeying without giving his consent. As he kept his consent outside the hold of the totalitarian regime, he remained faithful to himself. He forced himself to sacrifice everything but his "I." But one day, Winston was arrested by O'Brien. In his novel *1984*, George Orwell shows what forcing consent is.

"Get up," said O'Brien. "Come here."

Winston stood opposite him. O'Brien took Winston's shoulders between his strong hands and looked at him closely.

"You have had thoughts of deceiving me," he said. "That was stupid. Stand up straighter. Look me in the face."

He paused, and went on in a gentler tone:

> 'You are improving. Intellectually there is very little wrong with you. It is only emotionally that you have failed to make progress. Tell me, Winston-and remember, no lies: you know that I am always able to detect a lie-tell me, what are your true feelings towards Big Brother?'
> 'I hate him.'
> 'You hate him. Good. Then the time has come for you to take the last step. You must love Big Brother. It is not enough to obey him: you must love him.'[10]

This imperative pronounced by O'Brien, before leading Winston to room 101 where he will be tortured, indicates the point demanded by the Other of the totalitarian regime: the subject must give up on what he believes in, what he feels, his passions; he must love what he hates. Subjected to torture, Winston will yield, disowning his love for Julia. Such is the terror caused in his body by the rats that are in the cage, ready to devour his face, that he will eventually scream that he wishes torture would be applied to the woman he loves and not to him. He will yield to the terrorizing situation imposed on him by the militiamen. He will disavow his words, his personal history, his memories, his traumas, which he will henceforth consider false memories and erroneous recollections. He will be nothing more than this being with neither history nor subjectivity, utterly submitted to his executioner, subservient to the point of feeling love for his torturer.

Orwell then writes in capital letters one last sentence, the one which illustrates the abolition of the subject by forced consent. "THE STRUGGLE WAS FINISHED. HE HAD WON THE VICTORY OVER HIMSELF. HE LOVED BIG BROTHER."[11]

These are the paradoxes of a consent which is demanded from the subject, more particularly, in totalitarian regimes such as the Russian communist regime. What is ordered is the belief in the legitimacy of terror. It is the avowal, the public admission, the recognition before the people, which is demanded so that each and every one should be encouraged to kowtow to the "We" of fear and trembling. This requirement produces what Camus, in 1951, called: "ideologies of consent,"[12] namely discourses which extort consent from the citizens to make them bend under the yoke of a total power. Forcing the other to give his consent is typical of harassment and control under a totalitarian regime. One can glimpse here the risk inherent in the instrumentalization of "consent" in the political sense, namely, the risk of forcing a citizen to give his consent whilst he feels he has fallen prey to an authoritarian, dictatorial, and totalitarian regime. This misuse of consent at the service of an abuse of power is also a perversion applied to the subject's consent. For "To yield" to terror, intimidation and threats is not "to consent." With Camus, we see in what sense the "ideologies of consent" become "private and public techniques of annihilation."[13] They overstep voluntary servitude by articulating two contradictory terms: consent as an act of the subject, and awe and terror as they permeate the political climate incompatible with the genuine choice of a subject.

The blurring of the frontier between "to yield" and "to consent" is a distinctive feature of the totalitarian regime.

Notes

1 Hugo Grotius, *On the Law on War and Peace: Three Books*, 1625.
2 Frédéric Gros, *Disobey! A Philosophy of Resistance*, Transl. David Fernbach, 2020, Verso Books, 2020, p. 109.
3 Jean-Jacques Rousseau, *The Social Contract or Principles of Political Right*, Transl. G.D.H. Cole, public domain, p. 5.
4 Rousseau, *The Social Contract*, p. 15.
5 Rousseau, *The Social Contract*, p. 84.
6 Rousseau, *The Social Contract*, p. 3.
7 Rousseau, *The Social Contract*, p. 14.
8 Gros, *Disobey!* p. 110.
9 Albert Camus, *The Rebel: An Essay on Man in Revolt*, Transl. Anthony Bower, Vintage, 1992, p. 87.
10 George Orwell, *Nineteen Eighty-Four*, Modern Classics, 2013, p. 318.
11 Orwell, *Nineteen Eighty-Four*, p. 336.
12 Camus, *The Rebel: An Essay on Man in Revolt*, p. 123.
13 Camus, *The Rebel: An Essay on Man in Revolt*, p. 123.

Chapter 5

Shy of Consenting, "letting it happen"

I would like to come back to intimacy, to consent as the subject's intimate act.

To further examine the distinction between "yielding" and "consenting," I will use a third verb which is in the passive form: "to let it happen [*se laisser faire*]." To explore this frontier, which is thin but real, I will avail myself of the expression "to let it happen," as a link between "to yield" and "to consent." It is perhaps at the heart of this strange experience where "I let it happen," that the very possibility of a tipping-point occurs. "Letting it happen" in the sense of "submitting oneself to the other" may lead me towards a gentle "drifting along," just as it may place me in a situation where "I let myself be taken advantage of" by the other. In sexual and psychological trauma, a dimension of "letting it happen" comes into play and instils doubts since, for a split second, something like the passivity of the subject has rendered the abuse possible.

Why did I let it happen? On occasion, when it isn't an instance of total submission to physical force, whosoever has let it happen, could have reacted, resisted, or run away instead of letting it happen. The subject who submits himself or herself to another, "seems" therefore to consent to obscure intentions as if they submitted themselves to the other to learn what the other aimed at, aware that it is already too late to escape the situation. As if they gave the other an opportunity to get a grip on themselves, to stop before it was too late, and to pretend that nothing had happened, and the veil had not been torn.

Everything becomes confused then. If someone let it happen, it meant that they really wanted it, and that they consented. Their consenting to the situation means that they wished it to happen, even though it eventually traumatized them. It means that their being silent, passive, nonresistant was a "yes," an assent. Why didn't they say anything? How can we possibly know for sure? Is "to let it happen" a modality of will? Only a clinical approach of consent, based on what Freud and Lacan taught us, will enable us to distinguish between what concerns consent and what does not. Only the dimension of the unconscious, together with what Freud called the drive, can help us find our bearings in this labyrinth, where we move from consent to "letting it happen," before we get to a point where we finally lose our foothold and "yield" to the situation.

There are different degrees in "Letting it happen."

DOI: 10.4324/9781003536956-5

"letting it happen": Consenting to Let Go of Oneself

It is possible to "let it happen" first when it is one's desire that is at stake. This passivity relates to a letting go of oneself to which one has consented, a position adopted by the subject which does not abolish the subject. The jouissance traversing the body, within this experience of "submitting oneself to the other," is a jouissance which is consented to, welcomed, discovered as a delightful surprise.

In this first degree of "letting it happen," the subject "submits themselves to another" whom they desire. "Submitting oneself to another" does not crush the subject since it rests upon a "yes," an agreement with what is going on in the subject's body. It is a subjective possibility in the relation to the Other, in love mostly. It is not a submission but a consented submissiveness. A temporary, short-lived submissiveness accompanied by a certain experience of jouissance of one's body under the effect of the other's gestures. That would be the first degree in "letting it happen," the degree which ultimately involves a subject's choice, the choice of a form of momentary passivity offered to the other. This choice may be conscious or unconscious, what matters is that it is rooted in the subject's desire and that the subject recognizes himself or herself in it. It is a fully accepted passivity.

This passivity is what Annie Ernaux testifies to in her book *Simple passion* [*Passion simple*]. For a few months, she lived out a passion with a foreigner as she let her encounter with him turn her life upside down, without ever asking him anything, without ever expecting anything from him but his physical presence.

"From September last year, I did nothing else but wait for a man: for him to call me and come round to my place."[1] Giving up all her activities, withdrawing from the outside world, a woman submits herself to the love encounter. A passion she experiences almost without a word. An encounter of two bodies. "Now I was only time flowing through myself."[2] Waiting for this man, meeting him again, making love, let him go, and again wait for him to come back, next time, starting all over again, with the encounter of the bodies repeating itself. "I would slip into a semi-slumber which gave me the sensation I was sleeping in his body. The following day I would enter a state of apathy, forever reliving a caress he had given me or repeating a word he had spoken."[3] To submit oneself to passion is thus to embrace this lethargy of the body after the encounter, a lethargy which is what there is left afterwards, together with a feeling of strangeness.

In her account, Annie Ernaux pays tribute to what she discovered about herself through this man whom she will probably never see again, as she consented to welcome the encounter, which by definition is always contingent. "I discovered what people are capable of, in other words, anything: sublime or deadly desires, lack of dignity, attitudes and beliefs I had found absurd in others until I myself turned to them. Without knowing it, he brought me closer to the world."[4] This simple passion is a gift she received from life. While experiencing this encounter, writing is a means for her to list "the signs of a passion,"[5] which was also marked by silence. This passion took place outside the real world. With this man she shared nothing but their meetings. She also concealed what she was living from the people close to her. It was as if the time of the event, speech itself, were absorbed by passion. Ultimately, what the writer relates is the story of a *ravishing*. To submit oneself to this chance encounter, to love and desire, without expecting anything else from it, is what lies at the core of this book which bears the trace of a kind of destitution. In the end, she was nothing more than a woman waiting for a man, yet to this experience she consented heart and soul.

This first degree "letting it happen" is in tune with "consenting." The subject lets go of himself or herself, experiencing the disruption caused by the love encounter.

"letting it happen": Worrying about the Other's Desire

This is not however the only manifestation of "letting it happen," I can also let it happen while sensing that my passivity is a choice which is not without a feeling of anxiety as regards what the other wants from me. I would now like to define the second degree in "letting it happen" which has something to do with a question expressed to another. Here, I let it happen, I submit myself to the other in the sense that I comply with the other's request, to see what they really want, how far they can go, who they actually are. Yet I am worried. This second degree does not necessarily involve desire, but rather hinges on a form of anxiety. I submit myself to see, to know, to gamble on a relationship based on trust, but also to show the other what he or she desires, what part of their desire they take responsibility for, and what part they do not. As if the other's intentions could reveal themselves all the better as I submit myself to their desire.

One will never know if Camille really loved Paul. What one does know is that she asks him if he loves her, if he loves her body and her way of being. We will never know why she complied and consented to get into the producer's car alone, whilst it was Paul who should have accompanied her by taxi, from the Cinecitta Studios to the villa. We will never know exactly what happened during the journey.

To recount this episode, Jean-Luc Godard chooses two long scenes showing Camille's look and hair. First the look. Hers is a beseeching look towards her lover. Camille stares anxiously at Paul and before getting into the car, she even begs him to come with her: "Paul! Come." This takes place under the observation of the producer himself. It is a muffled request which already fractures something of Camille's intimacy. All of which occurs while the producer is looking at them.

Paul looks down, pretends he does not understand, keeps Camille waiting; she is caught between Prokosch's impatience and Paul's cowardice. Her lover behaves as if nothing important was happening, as if she was not risking anything, as if it was normal to let her get into the car alone with the other man, without saying a word. At that moment, Camille's look conveys distress and perhaps a breaking point too. It says: "Are you sure Paul, you want me to acquiesce in this?"

Paul is no longer present for her. Without a word, he leaves her to another man. He has consented to give her away.

Was she already dishevelled when she got into the producer's car? Was her splendid blond hair fastened by a dark headband above her forehead, already tangled? When Camille joins Paul at the villa, she doesn't so much as glance at him. Yet Jean-Luc Godard shows us this dishevelled hair by filming Camille, played by Brigitte Bardot, with her back turned and her hair undone, in the garden of the stylish villa. Godard presents the scene for us in a long take. Or is it perhaps Paul's look at Camille that we see? The slightly tousled hair allows doubt to linger. Camille' s avoidance of Paul's gaze, Paul's cycling from the Studios to the villa, his questioning – you took your time, didn't you? – his own silence, all this is enough to reveal what happened to Camille.

In his 1963 film, *Contempt*, Jean-Luc Godard plunges us at the heart of a couple's unravelling relationship.

Why such contempt and discord among human beings, set against gorgeous places, in contrast to the magnificent shots of the Capri Island, the view on the Casa Malaparte, and the sea on the horizon? Boredom, weariness, silence, unspoken words, contempt. Who despises whom by the way?

The film opens onto a superb, mythical sequence, where Camille, lying naked on a bed beside Paul – played by Michel Piccoli-, speaks of this body that he sees, her own body, for him, in the mirror. Looking at her feet, she calmly asks him if he loves her feet, "yes, he loves them," if he loves her thighs, "yes he also loves her thighs," if he loves her behind, "yes, I do," if he loves her mouth, "her mouth too," "yes," says Paul. He loves each part of her body. "So, you love me totally?" Camille answers. Yes, he loves her totally, from head to toe.

The film does not start with contempt [*mépris*] but with misunderstanding [*méprise*]. Does Paul love Camille totally just because he loves each part of her body? Or because he answers "yes" to her questions? Paul may be somebody who always consents to say "yes" without really meaning it, without really believing what he says. Although he answers Camille's questions, his mind seems to be elsewhere, he is perhaps engrossed in the screenplay he must write for a film shot by somebody else. Camille questions him as if to know where he is and who she really is for him.

Paul has been invited by Jeremy Prokosch (played by Jack Pallance), the producer of the film directed by Fritz Lang, to join him in his villa in the area around Cinecitta. When he reaches the Studios with Camille, he lets her get into the car with the producer. Was this planned? Why should Camille find herself alone with another man who is a decision maker, whose financial means exceed Paul's, and who has the upper hand over the film? Must he also have the upper hand over his wife?

Godard films Camille staring at Paul a second time when the scene recurs in Capri and Paul lets her get into the boat alone with the other man. At that moment, anxiety is also reflected in her eyes as she is asking him: "Are you coming Paul? Paul? Paul? This moment contradicts and disclaims the opening scene. Paul loves this body totally, yet he is not particularly keen on keeping Camille for himself. This is what Camille discovers for a moment, in Rome, before opening the door of the convertible and sitting down within easy reach of the other man, and a second time in Capri before getting into the boat.

Camille's eyes, as filmed by Godard, convey a kind of distress; it is as if she was saying to him "don't leave me with him," "don't barter me for your scenario." But Paul does not answer and acts as though he didn't understand. Under her gaze, in front of her, he consents to hand her over to the producer, behaving as if nothing had happened. Similarly, under the producer's authority, he consents to rewrite another's screenplay, that of Fritz Lang who is shooting his *Odysseus*.

There, as Paul no longer says anything, the saying "silence is consent" finds its place, a different place from the one I mentioned earlier regarding trauma. Here it is the "silence is consent" of a man whose silence means: "yes, I accept that you get into the car." The absence of words from Paul reveals his consent to leave Camille to the producer. Such consent verges on cowardice. It is the "Silence is consent" of the coward who falls silent to conceal his consent. Paul lets Camille get into the producer's car as if he did not know what was going to happen, as if nothing special was taking place. And yet he knows. At that precise moment, Camille complies. She calls Paul as if to ask him: "Is it what you really want?" as if to confront him with his non-desire and she eventually submits herself to his non-response.

She submits herself to Paul's silence.

Paul must write the screenplay of a film called *Odysseus*. It is a new version of the Homeric tale which contradicts Ulysses' and Penelope' story by questioning Penelope's faithfulness. What if Penelope had betrayed Ulysses? What if Ulysses, rather than being prevented from coming back to Penelope, took all his time and came back to Ithaca as late as possible because he does not feel like coming back. Thus, the screenplay reverses Homer's tale, turning the woman into a traitor and Ulysses into a man who is detached from his wife, as if the odyssey became the odyssey of this detachment. As if Homer's epic poem also recounted the story of a couple who falls apart.

If Camille submitted herself to Prokosch, isn't it because ultimately, she agreed with Paul on the fact that it was already over between them? One will never know. But Camille, a kind of Penelope who no longer expects anything from Ulysses, chooses not to say anything to him, ever. She chooses silence. Where Paul despised her by bartering his wife for a cheque, Camille despises Paul. She no longer speaks to him. She doesn't say anything to him. Her silence is the sign of her contempt. She leaves him with his consent and his cowardice. If Camille complied, it was because she wanted to know whether Paul loved her or not. She no longer needs to ask him if he loves her body, she now knows that he does not care about her as a woman.

At the end of the film, Camille only tells him one thing before leaving with Prokosch: "I despise you Paul." I am leaving because I despise you. He will try to know or rather will pretend that he does not know and does not understand why: "Is it because I let you get into the producer's car?" Camille does not answer, and Paul knows very well that Camille does not need to answer him. "It is because I despise you Paul." Camille will not give him any other reason and will not blame him either. They won't quarrel. Paul no longer exists for Camille. Where he despised her, she despises him for being the man who has shown contempt for their love. Where he consented to hand her over to another man, for a script which he doesn't manage to write, another man she finally gives herself to, she despises him for his cowardice. She despises his silence.

The film ends with the word "*Silencio*" opening the scene onto the open sea. The end.

Camille's complying with Paul's request at the end of the film can be seen as an act. She has returned Paul's contempt as she chose to leave with the producer. We will never know if she loves this man but what we know is that she no longer loves Paul and that she will never be able to love him again. Camille's passivity when Paul lets go of her and since the moment when his cowardice was silently brought to light is somehow a means to reveal a truth. Camille has brought out Paul's passivity, his absence of desire, his way of giving in without seeming to do so. Paul does not love her. Her compliance has turned against him. She drew strength from it. She leaves him alone, imprisoned in his own silence. Without her.

Camille is a paradoxical feminine character, who complies while at the same time having the strength to take responsibility for the separation, in his place. She will not yield to Paul's questions. She will not tell him the truth. By keeping quiet, she regains possession of herself. She won't enter a discussion with him about what happened to him, about Paul's responsibility, his cowardice, his love. She will only tell him: "I despise you," you who made me believe that you loved me totally while in fact you took advantage of me for a film, you who talked to me about love while for you, I was just an object you could barter. Camille returned Paul's contempt towards him by keeping quiet and leaving with the other man, which is what Paul wanted and what he consented to make possible.

With this radiant and mysterious film, I point out a very singular meaning of "letting it happen" in the sense of "complying," which brings a truth to light. "Complying" in this context is an act, showing the other something, in silence, while it also involves a kind of suffering. Camille's compliance is also an encounter with suffering, yet the experience does not confine her to a state of passivity. It enables her to bring to light the truth of what she is to Paul.

This "letting it happen" is a real question addressed to the Other: what do you want for us? What are you prepared to do so that what unites us should not be destroyed? Paul is not ready to let the script and the prospect of a cheque slip away. His cowardice leads him to pretend that what is happening to his love, to their couple, this detachment, has nothing to do with his behaviour.

"letting it happen": Yielding to Terror

I will now move on to the third degree in "letting it happen," which somehow involves more suffering for the subject. I will deal with "letting it happen" in trauma. Immersing oneself with the subject in the period preceding the trauma means creating a freeze-frame where the subject submits themselves to the other, yielding to the situation, in other words, where he or she is unable to respond. Here, I would like to broach another register.

I want to immerse myself into this blurred and obscure moment when the subject is no longer able to consent or not. There and then, must the phrase "silence is consent" be refuted because silence takes on another meaning: it means you are no longer able to say a word, that you are cut off from the world of speech on account of the effraction caused by the traumatic situation in your body; you are petrified. She was only eight when it happened. She was unable to speak. She yielded in silence. Emma is a little girl who loves sweets. She occasionally goes out shopping. She is wearing a dress, the dress of an eight-year-old girl. She walks into the grocery store to buy sweets. She knows that the grocer sells sweets. So, she enters the shop by herself, wearing her small dress. And there, something happens which she could not in the least expect. She doesn't even have the time to feel anxiety. It just happened, and she couldn't say a word. The grocer looked at her and he may have even smiled at her in a funny way, the way an old man smiles, attracted as he was by the young girl who had just entered his shop of her own free will. Why should he deprive himself of pleasure? What does the old man do? He probably finds her pretty and ingenuous to come to the shop on her own to treat herself to sweets. He is going to make her try something else without her understanding anything. Suddenly, as the little girl is standing there opposite him, with the sweets in her hands, he draws near her, and "grabbed at her genitals through her clothes."[6] Emma is petrified. Can we say that she let it happen? She said nothing, did not budge, paralyzed as she was by what was taking place. She probably did not have time to run away. But, most importantly, she understood nothing. The time of anxiety has been short-circuited. This time which also signals a danger did not take place. Anxiety was not experienced. She was not even worried before walking into the shop precisely because she was happy to go there to buy the sweets she was so fond of. Did she go to the grocery secretly? Had she told her mother or her father that she would go there? Maybe she didn't. Maybe she did not tell anyone, which was the reason why she found herself trapped. She had come there to indulge in sweets, a pure child's pleasure. She may have stolen a coin from her mother's purse to be able to afford the sweets she loved. Alone, defenseless, and without protection. She finds herself under the yoke of an adult who sees an opportunity to satisfy a drive: touching the little girl's genitals through her dress. She lets it happen.

Freud met Emma when she was already a young woman "subject [...] to a compulsion of not being able to go into shops *alone*"[7] without really knowing why. This is what there is left from that day, when she was only eight years old, now that she has grown up, and her body has been transformed. But she has no recollection of that moment when she yielded to the situation. It is amnesia. She has forgotten. Emma, the subject, has forgotten the eight-year-old girl's trauma. What the young woman who addresses Freud remembers is another event which happened to her when she was 13 years old. For her, this memory conjures up a more recent past, a time in her life when her body had reached puberty. She knew then that she was no longer a child and that she could be stared at with desire. This memory has to do with an event related to a shop she entered and where something untoward happened. She remembers that she had walked into a shop at the age of 13 to buy something, but she ran away at once. Odd. Nothing happened in the shop except that the two shopkeepers looked at her and laughed. Was there something ridiculous about her? Was it her outfit, her dress, her body? Emma came out of the shop, panicking. She felt humiliated. Both men seemed to make fun of her, of her dress and of her body. She was all the more embarrassed as she found one of them attractive. Emma ran away. Freud underlines the enigmatic aspect of Emma's symptom: to be haunted by the idea that she should by no means walk into a shop on her own and remembering the two shop-assistants who burst out laughing when they saw her, when she was 13. This is not enough to justify this anxiety which takes hold of her each time she walks into a shop and above all to account for the presence of this fixed idea. What is this compulsion? As she is talking to Freud, Emma will one day remember what she had forgotten, what happened to her child's body when she was eight. It is precisely when she remembers the other memory, the one summoning up the traumatic episode which occurred when she was eight, that Emma can start to undo the threads of her symptom.

At 13, she could not remember at all that the scene she had just relived with the two shop-assistants echoed another one, an older scene which had left her speechless. But talking to Freud of shops, clothes, assistants, brought back to the surface what she had forgotten. It enabled her to untie the knots of time. Her own knot, where the older event was kept hidden inside the more recent one, as if to remind her of its presence whilst at the same time lying low. So, what does she remember? Not only does she remember the first time, the moment when the grocer grabbed at her genitals through her dress, but she also remembers something else, something so strange. What she can say to Freud is that she had entered the shop twice, and that the abuse did occur the first time. Why did she go back to the shop a second time?

Freud writes: "She now reproached herself for having gone there the second time, as though she had wanted in that way to provoke the assault."[8] She went a second time into the shop, knowing. If something happened the first time because she did not know, the second time confronts her with the mystery of what she knew. How can this return to the scene of the trauma be read? Is it Freud who adds "as if she had wanted to provoke the assault?" or is it Emma who asks herself "why did I go back?" What we know is that she went back to the scene of the trauma where she had experienced an effraction in her body which left her speechless. What Freud wants to show first concerns the removal of amnesia. How can psychoanalysis help recover a repressed memory? How is it possible that, what has never been said so far, should be revealed not only to the other but to herself? For trauma always goes hand in hand with silence. The subject who couldn't say a word at the time can't say a word afterwards either. As if the mouth had been irrevocably sewn shut on the event. Freud therefore focusses on the way the first memory was repressed, and on this "deferred" [après-coup] mechanism which shows that a second scene is necessary for the first one to emerge.

What is the path that led her to reencounter the first time of the trauma?

The second episode which took place when she was 13 repeats something of the first scene without being identical to it. But when this second episode occurs, she does not remember anything. It is when she talks about this second episode to Freud allowing herself to say whatever comes to her mind at the thought of the obsessive fear of entering a shop alone, that she discovers the first erased memory by accident. Emma finds echoes of the former memory through the latter: the shop, entering by herself, the clothes (the assistants' laughs supposedly linked to her outfit) and an effect on her body – she finds one of the assistants attractive. What holds Freud's attention is this temporal duality. "A memory is repressed which has only become a trauma by *deferred action*."[9] The "après-coup"[10] is the moment when the first trauma reveals itself through a second one. The scene Emma remembered, which occurred when she was 13 years old, will constitute – retroactively – the first scene, initially marked by a blank, a gap, a trauma. What was missing from the first episode was the emergence of anxiety. Instead of anxiety and short-circuiting anxiety, there was an effect of intrusion into her body. The child experienced something she had never experienced before, while remaining speechless. Because there had been an effraction.

Silence, amnesia, effraction – such are the three features which characterize sexual trauma.

Anxiety appeared much later and turned into a symptom – the obsessive fear of entering a shop on her own.

The trauma is a consequence of the child yielding to the situation. But when it occurred, she was not there as a subject. It was her body that went through something she did not understand. This is what I would call the third stage of "letting it happen" which has little to do with the first ones already mentioned, the first related to consent and the second to demand and anxiety.

The question I would like now to ask is one that could bring some valuable insight into the significance of "letting it happen" in this third degree. Why did the eight-year-old child go back to the shop, even though she had fallen victim to an abuse? How should we interpret this repetition?

Freud underlines the fact that Emma blamed herself for going back there as if she had wanted it to happen again. This is indeed an enigma. In 1897, Freud cannot yet avail himself of the repetition compulsion theory. Only twenty years later, in his article entitled "Beyond the Pleasure Principle," will he be able to relate the drive to repetition and account for this return, for what comes back in the body, without the subject.

So why does Emma go back then? What I will point out is, on the one hand, the first moment, of a "letting it happen" in the sense of "yielding," before which she is utterly defenseless and on the other hand, a second moment, when she "goes back," it being the first effect of the trauma. But the question to be explored is "why does she go back?" There lies the fundamental difference between "yielding" and "consenting." Does she go back to yield to the situation again? I would not interpret it that way. The eight-year-old-girl goes back to the shop, but this time she knows what can happen there, even if she can't say anything about it. It is a knowledge that comes from her body.

Yet, this impossibility to say may be linked with this return. She goes back there without knowing what she has lost. So, when we lose something somewhere, without knowing why, what do we do? We go back to the scene to try and find out what we have lost and perhaps to retrieve it. What is certain is that something happened to her, and that she can't go back in time. This return is somehow a repetition of the conditions of what happened as if to make sense of it. After this traumatic instant of seeing, she returns to see again what she was unable to understand. My hypothesis is that she goes back there to retrieve what has been torn away from her, a turmoil in her body before the body had reached puberty. Where the eight-year-old child was unable to react as the grocer moved his hand towards her body, there is now a movement towards the place where she had remained petrified. This movement can be read as a commemoration of the trauma. What she is looking for is not the grocer who grabbed her genitals through her dress; she wants to relive the scene that left her speechless. This logic is relevant to the loss which has marked the child's body. She goes back precisely because the trauma has remained a violation against her body.

"Yielding" in trauma engenders a repetition compulsion even before it constitutes itself as a trauma for the subject. When the subject yields, he is somehow trapped by the trauma which has torn his body from him. Only many years later, when she is 13, will Emma experience the anxiety she could not experience when she was 8. This deferred anxiety is the signature of trauma.

This last degree of the "letting it happen" which Freud identifies at the origin of psychoanalysis, and which causes psychological trauma, is also the one that produces a blank in the subject's memory. A "censored chapter of one's history," as Lacan later will say of the unconscious, trauma is outside the domain of what can be said and transmitted. It becomes for the subject a kind of navel, a mysterious kernel which remains unsayable. The passivity of trauma cannot be symbolized.

"Whosoever is silent," in this case, is destined to return to the scene as if to recover the speech lost where the abuse took place. Whosoever is silent does not understand what happened and tries to rediscover this body, which was prematurely awakened to a turmoil, leaving the subject beset by anxiety.

What lies shy of anxiety? Perhaps the disgust of her own body which was instrumentalized by the other in this way. Perhaps the shame of this body which aroused somebody else's jouissance? Perhaps some indifference for the transformation of this body that she had to recognize as hers at a moment when it had become so foreign to her.

Notes

1 Annie Ernaux, *Simple Passion*, Transl. Tania Leslie, Fitzcarraldo Editions, 2021, p. 2.
2 Ernaux, p. 8.
3 Ernaux, p. 9.
4 Ernaux, p. 35.

5 Ernaux, p. 14.
6 Sigmund Freud, "Project for a Scientific Psychology", in *The Standard Edition of the Complete Psychological Works of Sigmund Freud*, Transl. James Strachey, Vol. I, Vintage Classics, London, 2001, p. 353.
7 Freud, p. 353.
8 Freud, p. 354.
9 Freud, p. 356.
10 *Nachträglichkeit* [TN].

Chapter 6

Yielding "on"

The three degrees in the "letting it happen," which I have just distinguished – "let it happen" in keeping with a subject's choice (passionate love), "let it happen" deriving from a subject's question (Camille in Godard's film *Contempt*), and "let it happen" which goes against the subject's desire (Emma's case when she was eight) – allow me to move towards the question of the body. This is the place where the "yielding" that is not "consenting" leads us, a place where the body yields to something while the subject remains dumbstruck. This is the point I am reaching, where "whoever is silent" finds themselves transfixed with fright, petrified, literally turned into a stone body. The frozen body of the traumatized subject undergoes an effraction which leaves him unable to speak.

So, what does experiencing turmoil and dread in one's body without consenting mean? "Yielding" is the body's response where there is no response from the subject, when it is impossible for the subject to say anything. "Yielding" is giving up.

Something splits, cracks open, breaks apart, and gives way. The subject is reduced to ashes.

Let's move towards the tragic territory of trauma. We have seen how sexual and psychological trauma is at the heart of Freud's elaboration as he discovered the unconscious. The silence of the subject and the emergence of a strange repetition which leads one to go back to the scene of the trauma constitute, Freud argued, the stigmata of the trauma.

To Yield on One's Desire

What would the Lacanian contribution be to our aphorism "yielding is not consenting"? Lacan has given a specific place to the verb "yield" in the psychoanalytical language. This place is even so specific that the Lacanian catchphrase where the verb "yield" is to be found has become a kind of slogan in psychoanalysis,[1] the hallmark of the ethics of psychoanalysis according to Lacan. This catchphrase is not about trauma but upon the relation to desire. It comes up at the end of the seminar dealing with "The Ethics of Psychoanalysis." In 1960, Lacan ends his yearly teaching by unveiling the aim of psychoanalysis. An analysis is not a promise of happiness, nor does it lead one to look on the bright side of life. However, it makes

DOI: 10.4324/9781003536956-6

access to desire possible. Lacan therefore argues that "The only thing of which one can be guilty, at least in the psychoanalytical perspective, is of having yielded on one's desire."[2] In other words, he establishes a link between guilt and desire, and, in an unheard-of way, connects desire to a surprising use of the verb "to yield."

Lacan admittedly uses this verb in an unusual sense. In everyday language, the French verb *"céder"* (to yield) is followed by the preposition *"à"* [to]. For example, *"céder à la tentation,"* "to give in to temptation." Now, what is surprising is that Lacan, by saying "céder sur" (yield on) gives the verb *"céder"* [yield] a new, if not unexpected meaning. What does "to yield on one's desire" mean? It means exactly the opposite of "giving in to one's desire." "To yield on one's desire" does not mean to let oneself be tempted by the delights of desire and jouissance; on the contrary, it means to "give ground relative to one's desire," to abandon it, to give it up, to forget it and to try to bury it. By the same token Lacan gives a new value to "desire." Desire is neither pleasure nor drive, even though it can meet with these two dimensions. Desire is what each of us profoundly aspires to, regarding one's being and the realization of one's being. Paradoxically, this desire demands that one should give a lot of oneself.

Lacan wants us to be aware that desire is precarious and fragile and that it can easily be crushed. It is always tempting to give it up, to "yield on one's desire." It is therefore up to the subject to acknowledge the existence of his or her desire, to defend it and not to let go of it, since there will always be good reasons in life to give it up and to make no room for it at all. The relation to desire must not be taken for granted. Whoever does not invest himself or herself in their desire cannot hope to encounter it. In other words, the subject is alone to save his or her desire. Nobody can do it in their place. There is something I can't let the other do in my place. And, to some extent, this new meaning of "letting it happen" also implies giving up one's desire, betraying it, yielding on it, giving ground on it. In fact, letting it happen to the point of betraying one's desire is at a level that could be placed between the second degree (letting it happen in the sense of complying, so that the other can show his or her true feelings) and the third degree (letting it happen, yielding under the effect of trauma). Here, it would be a question of a "letting it happen" which also means "letting the other decide what I want." This dimension, which leads to "giving ground relative to one's desire," is the one which results in dismissing the value of one's desire by favouring other obligations which seem more legitimate from the other's point of view. It is precisely in the name of what Lacan calls the service of goods, namely obligations which are in no way relevant to desire, that we dismiss our desire by trampling upon it.

I alone can make my desire into a value which governs my existence. If I wait for the other to acknowledge it as a legitimate desire before caring about it, I will wait a long time. So, I am also responsible if I don't act according to my desire. I desire, therefore I am. Such could be the principle of the Lacanian cogito. Yielding on one's desire is betraying oneself. It is yielding on one's being.

However, the Lacanian conception of desire is not a simple-minded approach. Desire is not everything that I fancy, that tempts me or that awakens the drive.

If this were the case, the Lacanian aphorism could be distorted and wrongly used by Sadean morality which states that one must never renounce jouissance. Now, for Lacan, desire is not jouissance.

Desire is not an invitation to brave the impossible either. It is not to believe that everything is possible and end up banging your head against the wall of the impossible. Desire is therefore not an excuse for escaping the world as it is. This ode to desire with which Lacan ends his seminar *The Ethics of Psychoanalysis* is not an invitation to enjoy without constraints nor is it an invitation to ask for the impossible. When Lacan states that ethics consists in "not yielding on one's desire," he doesn't mean that one should desire the impossible, whatever the cost. So, he does not say that anything is possible because it is not. And it is even by making room for what is not possible, the impossible, that desire can thread its way through the existence of a human being, taking into account the contingencies that may occur.

Choosing One's Desire, an Unconditional Will

But why then should he use the word "to yield on?" It is not a here a question of consenting to desire as in the field of love, but a question of "not yielding on one's desire." This wording almost points to a relation to desire which is poles apart from consent. This expression introduces a relation to will, decision and choice, in desire, which seems to be more than a mere consent. In short, it is a matter of "choosing desire," once we catch a glimpse of it, as we choose one moral value rather than others.

If Lacan defines the ethics of psychoanalysis as "not yielding on one's desire," he does so to give this ethics a Kantian dimension, even though his ethics is totally opposed to Kant's moral philosophy. What is the definition of moral law in Kant's philosophy? The rigour of the moral law is what leads one to do one's duty even if it means suffering because one must ignore one's feelings, interests and inclinations. You must do your duty whatever happens, whatever you feel: such is the spirit of the Kantian moral, which is inflexible and unconditional. What Kant considers a good will is good in so far as it wants the moral law as if it were its own good, while as a matter of fact it is the good of all, or rather, the good from the perspective of reason and the universal. This good will is what is at work when I am doing my duty. The ethics of psychoanalysis is about making of desire an unconditional value, a value which is as imperative as Kant's moral law. One must be prepared to sacrifice all that stands in the way of this value.

What Lacan retains from Kant before subverting it is this imperative dimension of the moral law, which is also the characteristic of duty, an imperative dimension which has no exceptions. According to Kant, whatever the circumstances, whatever the state I am in, whatever the historical situation, I must submit myself to the moral law. I must consent to it as if to a dimension which goes beyond me. For the author of *Groundwork of the Metaphysics of Morals* and *The Critique of Pure Reason,* to yield is always "yielding to one's inclinations, "yielding to" one's feelings, yielding to the passions of the soul which for him are also illnesses of the mind. Concretely, moral action according to Kant must be as rationally necessary as the law of nature; you must keep your promises, you must never lie, you mustn't take your own life, such are the moral duties which impose themselves to us from the point of view of reason and tolerate no exception. In that respect, in the land of Kantian moral, the only thing one can be guilty of is of having yielded to one's inclinations.

Moving from "yielding to" to "yielding on," Lacan turns Kant's theory upside down. Where Kant locates the moral law, Lacan locates desire. Where Kant locates inclinations and feelings, Lacan locates the Superego and the drive. So, it is really a question of "not yielding," not "to" but "on." In psychoanalysis, each one is faced with the duty to respect, not the moral law, which commands, but desire, which says the being of the subject. In short, "Not yielding on one's desire" means not yielding to the drive. Where the demand of jouissance stands in the way of desire – which for Lacan is distinct from the drive – one must not "yield on one's desire," which means one mustn't downplay its importance, underrate its value, or underestimate it. It is precisely because desire emerges as a value which is added to life in a contingent way, that one must not neglect it. Because without desire one's existence is distressing. One must not neglect it; one must listen to it. Paying attention to one's desire is having the courage to take into consideration its whisper, its murmur, its fragmented message. Desire does not give orders; it doesn't vituperate, nor does it ever yell. It expresses itself implicitly, its presence is quiet and discreet, as if to say to the subject: "I am here," "Do you want me?" "Do you want to pick me up?" "Do you want an existence in keeping with your desire or do you wish to conform to what society wants, to what the others value, to what can be easily obtained by submitting yourself and adapting to the norms of a standardized, anonymous life, to what is expected from you, to what seems to be the good according to the others?" Desire keeps asking me: "Deep down what do you really want?"

So, one of the distinctive features of desire is being the polar opposite of command. It is not desire that commands and imposes obedience through fear, it is the superego. Lacan puts the greatest distance between the superego, which is the ally of death, and desire. He even goes as far as asserting that this distancing between the two is an orientation for the subject. The more the subject keeps his or her death drive at a distance, the more they allow their desire to make its way through their lives.

Not Yielding to the Stranglehold of the Superego

Not yielding "on" one's desire is, in short, not yielding "to" the superego which never fails to betray desire. The superego is this authority within me which urges me to go along with what makes me suffer, which orders me to sacrifice my desire, whilst presenting itself as the Good, even the Sovereign good. What is dangerous about the superego is that it does not always seem austere and stern. It is not necessarily repressive. It may even present itself as an inner voice which keeps pushing me towards an ever more extreme jouissance as if this were the good I had to seek. Whether it drives me towards suffering or a limitless jouissance, the superego always leads me to the sacrifice of my desire. What the superego wants from me is that I should "yield on" my desire.

To sum up, the superego, which demands that I sacrifice my desire, is a sadistic authority in me which gives me a masochistic jouissance, one that makes me believe that I did good because I suffered from accomplishing something against my will. That is why Lacan draws a parallel between the cruelty of Kant's moral law – the imperative character of the moral duty – and Sade's cruelty – the demand of a limitless jouissance. It is in this suppression of all sentimental elements that Lacan unearths a secret affinity between Kant and Sade. In Sade, he sees the "first step of a subversion, of which [...] Kant represents the turning point."[3] The Sadean moral is that which upholds the "right of enjoyment over the other's body," whatever their consent and even without it. The Sadean character derives his jouissance from forcing consent.

The Sadean moral was reworded by Freud in *Civilization and Its Discontents* in 1929, as a death drive through which emerges, within the human being, the temptation towards the other to "satisfy their aggressiveness on him, to exploit his capacity for work without compensation, to use him sexually without his consent [*ohne seine Einwilligung*], to seize his possessions, to humiliate him, to cause him pain, to torture and to kill him."[4] Using the other sexually without their consent is not only to seek one's own enjoyment, following thereby a so-called hedonist moral, it is to satisfy a drive which is a drive for destruction. The latter can go as far as enjoying the annihilation of the other when nothing stops the search for the satisfaction of the drive. Connecting this injunction to enjoy without limits with the enigma that a woman's body can represent, Eric Laurent thus interprets "feminicide," which consists in killing a woman because she is a woman, in the light of the Sadean moral. "Feminicide" bears witness to the fact that, in the face of the enigma of sex, a demand for jouissance of a woman's body can be absolutized without limits."[5] In other words, the sexual use of the other's body without their consent particularly targets the body of this part of humanity whose consent is not based on a visible sign. To care about a woman's consent is to accept to decipher her desire, that is, it implies saying something to her and being able to take her response into consideration. Sadean moral, on the contrary, encourages to make of forcing a law to enjoy.

As Lacan recalls, with Sade, it is a question of a "free disposition of all women indistinctly whether they consent or not."[6] Which means that the right to jouissance knows neither limits nor boundaries, it is never-ending. And jouissance will be all the more intense since the other will be its victim.

Let's come back then to this death drive identified by Freud and to the Sadean superego defined by Lacan, to fully grasp the meaning of the formula about the ethics of psychoanalysis: "not to yield on one's desire." The superego as defined by Lacan, the superego which treats desire harshly, is an instance in each of us which wants to enjoy, whether the subject consents to it or not. I will therefore now address another dimension of the death drive, which is no longer the temptation to destroy the other, but the temptation to destroy oneself. Lacan's definition of the death drive as governed by the superego is of interest since it somehow situates the executioner and the victim within the same human being. The subject becomes his or her own executioner when they obey the superego's injunctions.

This is where I would describe the subject's consent in respect to the superego, as tarnished. This is also where psychoanalysis sheds a new light on the question of consent.

"*The Ethics Of Psychoanalysis*," with the Sadean rewording of the superego, is about a consent which is forced "by" jouissance. But what Lacan wants to emphasize is that this jouissance can also be mine, that it is jouissance that leads me to submit myself to the superego which is my own. Whether you consent to it or not, the superego wants you to experience jouissance by accomplishing what it commands you to accomplish. The superego grants himself the right to enjoy regardless of the subject's consent. This superego is an aspect of my being. Whether he consents or not, it wants to enjoy, enjoy repeatedly at the risk of carrying the subject to death.

I will now thus introduce a new degree in the "letting it happen," a "letting it happen" which implies a masochistic jouissance. As I progress in this attempt to decipher the enigma of consent, I am obliged to add elements to my first classification. I first distinguished three degrees in "letting it happen": consent to passion, a means to question the other's desire, a reaction to the traumatic event. I realize that between the last two degrees, I can introduce another two, which are also bridges between "to consent" and "to yield": "let it happen and submit to the other in order to please them and be loved by them at the risk of sacrificing my desire," "let it happen and submit to the Superego," which always urges one to choose jouissance over desire.

"Submitting to the superego" is therefore a dimension which can be located from the psychoanalytical point of view. In other words, submission to the other is possible only because the subject lets it happen although he does not desire it, that is, he yields *on* his desire. This desire is somehow sacrificed at the service of an anxious demand for love, an impossibility to escape the other's influence. Submission to the Other is intensified by a submission to the superego who says to the subject: "you must." You must do what it demands of you. You must satisfy it. You must try again and again until you succeed. There lies the foundation of the nightmare which renouncing one's desire constitutes, with its share of depressive affects: boredom, sadness, and sometimes even a disgust for life.

This is why an unrivalled force is needed to respond to the superego and keep at a distance the imperative of jouissance with its destructive force that never runs out. "Not yielding on one's desire" is somehow a psychoanalytical answer to the death drive in each one, such as is embodied in the superego. "Not to yield on one's desire" is not to submit to the superego – in the Kantian sense (that of the sacrifice of one's desire in the name of duty) or in the Sadean sense (that of the sacrifice of one's desire in the name of an unbridled jouissance).

The Meaning of Guilt Reversed

I said above that desire does not command. I will also add: "whoever commands never speaks to desire." "Whoever commands" without allowing the subjects to choose, "whoever orders" without taking the trouble to know what the other can and may want, is not concerned with consent but only with obedience, with submission even. He is concerned with what works and remains indifferent to what of the subject and his or her desire is in breach of what is ordered. Desire does not shout; it does not vociferate, nor does it give orders. Sweet, delicate and fair desire, you make yourself heard by whomever can listen carefully, beyond the sometimes deafening noise of the superego.

If it is not the language of morals or that of command, obligation, and sacrifice, what language then does desire speak, from the unconscious? Is it the language of love? Not exactly or if it is, then it is the language of love as a way towards something else. According to Lacan, desire distinguishes itself from love which can urge the subject to forget his or her desire, out of love or for love, and submit to the drive. Desire speaks a language which has to do with the language of love but in the sense of *eros*. Desire does not push you to become one with the other, it encourages you to realize your being. Desire speaks not to benumb the subject in a dream of romantic fusion, but to awaken him or her to themselves. Desire speaks genuinely, in a tone which acknowledges the being and does not despise it. It occasionally speaks in the middle of the night, through dreams that signal that something seeks recognition, that a message needs to be deciphered, that a desire is waiting to be articulated. When it is recognized and assumed, desire introduces a vital elan articulated with a meaning. Desire gives the subject a fulcrum to define his or her being and allows them to perceive what they really want and what they aim at for themselves.

Desire aspires to make itself heard, aims at being recognized, asserts its presence in an implicit way, weaves in and out of the subject's dreams and surprises of speech, as well as their slips of the tongue, to let him or her know that it is here and that it is possible to catch it, to realize it, to spread it out. Desire has to do with the secret history of the subject, his or her childhood, and the outline of his or her future. Concerning Freud, his most profound desire, the one on which he did not yield, was to discover how to interpret dreams. His own first, which presented themselves to him as the words of another. As for Lacan, his desire was to not allow psychoanalysis to yield to the demands inherent in the adaptation of the individual to some normality, by morphing into psychology. For each of them, the encounter with desire was possible on the condition that one should not yield to all that stood in the way, on the condition that one did not blame the other for giving up their desire, on the condition that one should believe in their desire and should want to know something about their destiny.

The ethics of psychoanalysis is then this regime of existence which leads one to knot one's life to one's desire as if to a new destiny, and not to the sacrifice of desire, to put one's work at the service of desire and not at the service of the values that crush desire. Nothing can justify the crushing of desire because desire is not harmful, on the contrary it is life-provoking. Yet, sometimes, to conform to the imperatives encountered in life in society – doing as the others do, not displeasing the others, submitting, conforming, obeying – the subject ruins and wastes his or her desire. One must have therefore the courage to disobey at times and not to fear losing the other's love, interest, and gaze, to make one's desire a Supreme Good. For that purpose, it is necessary to be sufficiently resolute so as not to bend before the cruelty of the superego who will inevitably and unfailingly encourage the subject not to take his or her desire into consideration and instead prefer the inaccessible ideal and the deadly jouissance.

Not to Betray Oneself

So, Lacan introduces an ascetic dimension where it is usually absent in classical morals. Psychoanalytical wisdom is the one that leads us to dedicate our lives to our own desire, one that encourages us to cultivate our desire and help it thrive and blossom. Where then is guilt located? What does the experience of an analysis allow us to discover regarding the guilt which we believe we feel about the other, for not doing enough, for not consenting to all possible efforts, for not being up to an ideal we have contrived for ourselves, for saying "no" sometimes to what the other expected from us?

When considered from the relation to the unconscious, guilt is discovered in a totally different place from conscious guilt. It also takes on another meaning. In Christian tradition, guilt is the result of a moral failing. The subject feels guilty of committing a sin. The failing related to the other leads to a reproach and even a self-reproach. One may sometimes even be led to think that the punishment will be deserved, and that punishment alone will make it possible to redeem oneself. So, there is a classical sequence which leads from sin to punishment through guilt. As if punishment was the only means to clear up guilt.

For Lacan, on the contrary, guilt is the sign of a moral failing committed towards oneself. It is no longer from a failing towards the other that the experience of guilt emerges, it is from a failing where my own desire is. It is because I yielded *on* my desire, because I sacrificed it to something else, that I feel guilty. I can't ignore my desire with impunity. My indifference to desire, my inclination to connive at my desire to forget about it, is what causes the feeling of guilt. I am to blame for damaging myself by dismissing my desire for the benefit of other good reasons.

The experience of an analysis would teach one to take one's desire seriously and not consider it as the fifth wheel of one's existence, as though it was superfluous to care about one's desire on top of the fundamental needs of life. "Not yielding on one's desire" is to have the strength to give one's desire as much value as if it were an intimate cause. It is to see that the sacrifice which must be made for the sake of desire is always worthwhile: whether it be the sacrifice of the goods, of interests, comfort, or the sacrifice of an aspect of the drive. Desire demands indeed that one should release oneself from what stands in its way. To take up Lacan's words, *a price must be paid for accessing desire.* Desire is never offered to jouissance as if all you had to do was to pluck it and make the most of it. It is up to me to decide, deep down inside myself, whether I want to bring it into existence or forget it. Not yielding "on" one's desire is to manage to sacrifice a part of jouissance, a part of habit, a part of passivity, a part of compulsive attachment, a part of symptomatic repetition, to give desire a chance to be realized. Desire can only become a power within me if I defend it in the face of other forces which are likely to crush it. It is never acquired once and for all, never to be taken for granted; one must take a chance on it again and again and stand up for it unrelentingly. Because, by definition, the world of the Other does not à priori seem conducive to the realization of my desire.

Not yielding "on" one's desire is thus to save one's being. But for Lacan, this never means to operate a forcing on the Other. Not yielding on one's desire is to be careful about one's jouissance. It is to jouissance that one has to say "beware." Because the drive will always seek to make its way through the paths of desire. Not yielding on one's desire is to not allow the demands of the drive to prevail over the advent of desire. If one must "not yield on," it is because another force urges us to "yield to." This power which can annihilate desire is the death drive in each of us, the force which seems to ignore the logic of desire and comes to answer in its place. For Lacan, the superego is the other name of the death drive, the moral disguise of this destructive force. This may be the place where the misunderstanding about what the ethics of psychoanalysis is, is to be found. That desire should stand poles apart of the superego does not mean that it goes in the direction of the drive, quite the opposite. The drive and the superego are on the same side. Desire alone is on the other side.

It is when I "yield" on my desire that I feel guilty because I have betrayed myself. I pretended that my desire did not mean anything for me. The ethical betrayal focusses on this point: "to yield on one's desire," to lack the courage to feel responsible for what makes me persevere in my being. This is where Lacan situates contempt, the other's and one's own.[7] Sacrificing one's desire under the other's pressure is despising one's being, renouncing oneself. Each one is then responsible for what he or she does with their desire, for the place and the strength they give it.

What model does Lacan choose to embody this act, "not yielding on one's desire"? Paradoxically, it is that of a tragic heroin who is heading for death. Antigone is nevertheless regarded by Lacan as the one who does not renounce her desire and turns it into a value which is larger than her own life. Sophocles' Antigone disobeys Creon who forbids her to bury her brother Polyneices who is a traitor to the country. But her disobedience is in the name of the affront she suffers, she cannot consent to leave her brother's body without covering it with dust to honour the dead man. She cannot consent to let the corpse of a member of her family be decomposed like the corpse of an animal. She cannot consent to remove the death of this brother from the symbolic dimension; this brother born from the same father and the same mother as she was, born from the same tragedy, that of their father's blindness.

Antigone neither consents nor yields. In short, she embodies this affinity between to yield and to consent but on the negative side. Not to consent, here and for her, is "not to yield." The young girl prefers to head for death, to be buried alive rather than give up her desire, which is to bury a brother afflicted by the same curse as she was, the curse of the Labdacids Dynasty.

Such a hopelessly willing victim, as Lacan put it. It is to show how far the power of "not yielding on" can go that Lacan chooses Antigone as an embodiment of desire, even though Oedipus' daughter is also the embodiment of misery. For her, the only good that exists is her desire, which is a desire not to yield, a desire to honour the dead brother, a desire to symbolize the loss of a brother by granting him a grave according to the laws of family and tradition.

"Not yielding on one's desire" can go as far as that: desire as an unconditional value must not be betrayed. If "to yield is not to consent," one could say however that here, "not to yield is not to consent." While in some respect, consent implies relying on the other, non-consent implies disobedience. Antigone does not submit to the laws of the city-state, she does not obey Creon, she does not abandon her cause. Never does she let it happen, in any way whatsoever.

Rather dying than "yielding on" one's desire.

Notes

1 Lacan's expression "céder sur son désir" was translated into English as "giving ground relative to one's desire" (*Seminar VII*, p. 311), whereas the verb "yield" was used in subsequent translations (e.g., *Seminar X*).

2 Jacques Lacan, *The Seminar of Jacques Lacan, Book VII. The Ethics of Psychoanalysis*, Ed. J.-A. Miller, Transl. Dennis Porter, W.W. Norton & Co., New York/London, 1992, p. 319.

3 Jacques Lacan, "Kant with Sade", in *Écrits. The First Complete Edition in English*, Transl., Bruce Fink, W.W. Norton & Co., London/New York, 2006, p. 645.

4 Sigmund Freud, "Civilization and Its Discontents", in *The Standard Edition of the Complete Psychological Works of Sigmund Freud*, Transl. James Strachey, Vol. XXI, Vintage Classics, London, 2001, p. 111.

5 Eric Laurent, "Comments on Three Encounters between Feminism and the Sexual Non-Relation", in *Psychoanalysis Lacan*, 5.

6 Jacques Lacan, *The Seminar of Jacques Lacan. Book VII*, "The Ethics of Psychoanalysis", Ed. J.-A. Miller, Transl. Dennis Porter, W.W. Norton & Co., London/New York, p. 79. Translation modified: "complete power over all women indifferently, whether they like it or not."

7 Lacan, p. 370.

Chapter 7

Yielding "to"

Is there any other use of the verb "to yield" in Lacan, which would lead me closer to the affirmation "yielding is not consenting" which I took as a starting point? The aphorism "To yield is not to consent" is becoming clearer as I wrote above, as one ventures into this opaque zone where the body yields without the subject consenting. It is then no longer a matter of desire and guilt, but a question of anxiety and the drive. It is no longer a matter of cowardice towards desire, one's own above all, but a question of an impossibility to escape the other's drive. From then on, the subjective dialectics no longer comes into play. It is precisely because one has been bypassed by the other as a desiring subject that trauma emerges, through abuse, harassment, and forcing.

A few years later, in 1963, Lacan gave the verb "to yield" a new value which, it seems to me, sheds a precious light on this frontier between to "yield" and to "consent." In his Seminar on *Anxiety,* Lacan connects the verb "to yield" not to desire but to the drive. There, the distinction between "yield" and "consent" grows drastically wider. Nothing allows one to bring them closer together. Lacan no longer uses "yield on,"[1] a word he was fond of in his 1960 Seminar *The Ethics of Psychoanalysis*, but "yield to." And there too he gives the expression to "yield to" a completely new meaning. It is not "yield to" temptation, or yield to a pleasure, or "to the other," after having hesitated, retreated, postponed, after feeling like saying "no," then "yes," or "yes but not immediately, not right now, not like this." No, it is about another "yielding to" which introduces the traumatic dimension.

We are no longer confronted to guilt but to anxiety. It is no longer a question of the subject, but of the subject in its relation to the body, to *his* or *her* body as a body of desire which also involves the drive.

What does the subject, deep down, yield to in sexual and psychological trauma?

A Traumatic Situation

The subject does not so much yield to the Other as to a traumatic situation against which he or she can't protect themselves. He or she yields to what is happening in their body. How is this to be understood? The danger is there, it is present, but the anxiety which could have signaled its presence was not experienced on time, the

DOI: 10.4324/9781003536956-7

effraction in the body having already taken place. It occurred too soon, and it is already too late. What the subject yields to is what he or she yields from themselves, what is taken from them of the way he or she as a living body is moved, stirred and affected. A part of their body is somehow torn from them *without* their consent, and it is the world of the Other which breaks up at the same time. The subject experiences a kind of earthquake, an upheaval which causes him or her to disappear. This brutal intrusion of the Other, via the gaze, the voice, a word that tears away the veil that covers the world of the bonds to the other, this intrusion, by targeting being and jouissance, through the body of the Other himself who imposes its drive and forces access, is the essential cause of the sexual and psychological trauma. Forcing access to jouissance means that it is the other's jouissance that imposes itself but, at the same time, it is also my own jouissance that is somehow taken away from a body which I have already lost.

In this "radical, traumatic confrontation, the subject yields to the situation,"[2] Lacan writes. It is not only a confrontation with the Other but also with a situation he or she is unable to live as a subject, because they don't have the means, whether psychological or physical, to face it. The traumatic situation is akin to a ravishment.

Lacan asks "what does it mean, at this level, at this moment to yield?"[3] He then introduces a crucial distinction between what can happen at the level of the subject himself or herself as a being of speech, and what can happen at the level of the subject's body, at the level of this body they have and which is not their being, while being what they have as most real.

Lacan's first answer is to dismiss what "yielding" is not. "It is not that the subject wavers or that he flags."[4] Wavering or flagging are modalities of being caught in the relation to the Other which have to do with "choice" and are, ultimately, modalities of "consent." To waver or flag is finally to let go of oneself to say "yes." It is no longer to deny somebody something or to refuse to surrender oneself to take the risk of living an experience with someone which will involve my body. But when it is a question of anguish and traumatic sexual situation, Lacan emphasizes that it is not on this register that this comes into play. Neither wavering nor flagging but "cession." What does this mean? Firstly, what is happening doesn't go through speech. It is not a contradiction, a refusal, or pressure. The "no" is a "no" of the body which is forced by the Other. Something of the subject became fixed in the situation. This is the "letting it happen" that occurred for eight-year-old Emma, who was petrified when the grocer, whom she had come to see because she wanted to buy sweets, grabbed at her genitals through her dress.

Fixity, an Impossibility to Say

"In a situation whose fixity puts right before our eyes its primitively inexpressible character, and by which he will remain marked forever, what occurred is something that gives its true meaning to the subject's *yield* – it's literally a cession."[5] Fixity, the unspeakable character of the traumatic situation, the body forever marked by the event, "cession."

What we find here is a description which plunges us at the heart of sexual and psychological trauma. "Fixity" first, which means the subject is somehow petrified. Their body, having become a body of stone, does not enable them to run away. Something of the living body has, to some extent, been ravished, extorted, and torn away from the subject. He or she no longer manages to extricate themselves from the situation. What must be emphasized here is that this ravishment is not only caused by a physical force against which I can't defend myself – which is also to be taken into consideration in the traumatic situation – but that below, this ravishment is caused by an explosion which affects the body in such a way that the subject is separated from this body, unable to move it. The subject is both reduced to his or her body which is trapped in the traumatic situation and compelled to yield something of their body.

An impossibility to say something about the traumatic situation. The subject is unable to say anything. His or her silence is not the silence of "Silence is consent," but rather it marks the impossibility for the subject to respond to the situation which he or she faces. They may scream, but they can't articulate a word. Or their speech will be nothing but a scream. This silence which occurs a first time will then be a stigmata of the traumatic experience that cannot be said. As if there was no possibility for speech to clear itself a way and speak about the traumatic situation. As if what was going to be repeated with the traumatic event was also this silence, a sort of impossibility to say something about it. I have already mentioned the strange temporality of trauma, with Freud and the case of Emma Eckstein, but also with the testimony and written account by Vanessa Springora. Thirty years of silence. It is not a contingency. Where the subject was unable to say something a first time, he or she will not be able to say anything afterwards.

This is in any case the conclusion I propose from the psychoanalytical perspective. In other words, what led to a sexual trauma is strangely redoubled by an "impossibility to say anything about it." As if a prohibition to speak about it had spread over what split open, what cracked in the world of the subject as he or she was confronted to the Other. The impossibility to say something about the traumatic situation thus produces a knot which keeps the event unspeakable. This "impossibility to say something about it" does not only depend on the historical or social context. This silence is also that which is engendered by the traumatic situation itself which short-circuited speech.

The "unspeakable" has several dimensions to it. First, the subject doesn't speak about it out of modesty. As though what he or she had experienced through forcing had left them with shame. As if the Other's jouissance had disgraced them too and had caused them to feel tarnished. Modesty is an affect which has a great value in one's existence and as a result one does not always wish to reveal what affected our body, what we have not grasped of what happened then in our flesh. We feel that talking about it to anybody would imply a new danger as if the traumatic rift was about to open again. Modesty is the affect which makes it possible in a way to deal with trauma without displaying it, by veiling it, by not using it publicly and maintaining it in the private intimate sphere which is not to be shared. Paradoxically, giving a particular value to the sexual trauma sometimes implies not sharing it with anyone but considering that specific conditions of speech will be needed to speak about it. It means considering that this is no ordinary event, but an event of another kind.

Trying to articulate a trauma always takes the dimensions of a confession. Now, to confess is not only to tell the truth, but also to try to say something about what has been experienced *without* the subject's consent. There lies the paradox. This confession may then weaken whoever fails to have what happened in their body acknowledged. This confession has no longer anything to do with truth but with what Lacan called "the real." What is at stake is not only the reality of what has taken place, but the effraction into a body, which is not of the order of what can be acknowledged in everybody's language but requires an immense trust in the person one addresses so that it can be said. An immense trust in their ethics, in their ability to listen to and believe you without judgement, in their capacity to welcome what is rejected. This impossibility to say the trauma refers to something unspeakable not merely situated at the level of what cannot be publicly communicated, but at the level of something intimate which is impossible to say. I will come back to it.

An Indelible Mark, Obsessive Fear

"Forever marked." This third detail noted by Lacan in his sentence about what "yielding to the situation" means, is crucial. It brings us back to the very origin of psychoanalysis. To what extent may there be indelible marks? Lacan's idea is that, if one keeps speaking in analysis, words – which, with Saussure, Lacan calls signifiers – end up crossing each other out to erase the previous words. If one keeps looking for the right word to say something about the traumatic core, the real of the event which took place for the subject seeks to write itself endlessly. The right words come then to mend the rift. Thanks to these words it is possible to circumscribe what has been taken away from the subject. But what can constitute a stopping point in this telling of trauma? Beyond all the words that can be said about one's suffering and one's history, there is also something which can't be erased, that one can't erase. Wishing to make a clean break with the past does not work with regards to the traumatic mark. It remains unaffected by words as well as by the passing of time. We can then, as I will show later, be presented with another relation to speech, no longer a speech which finds the repressed meaning but a speech bearing witness to the way the traumatic shock had its repercussions on the subject's relation to language itself.

Can one be forever marked by a traumatic event? Not only can this happen but this is the characteristic of psychological and sexual trauma. It is even the characteristic of trauma as such. A trauma is of the order of an effraction into the body which leaves a mark that can't be erased. Indelible. What is the use then of talking about it, one could ask? Is it not preferable to remain silent? Trauma confronts us with the fact that speech, in analysis, has several aspects to it. An aspect by which it enables us to remember, to retrieve pieces of our history – often from our childhood –

which had disappeared; it is an aspect through which it becomes possible for us to weave the history of a subject made of the turning-points that correspond to the traumatic events we have gone through.

The first effect of psychoanalysis is therefore of the order of "you can say." "Here you can speak of what seems to you to be rejected elsewhere." "Here we believe you. Here your words will not be suspected of lying." It is an aspect of the aphorism "Victims we believe you," which the collages against feminicides showed us over the walls of our cities in France. But with a grammatical change of person. Victims are no longer in the plural form and whoever believes is not an anonymous "we," In the experience of an analysis, what is encountered is a person who listens and says: "I believe you."

The dimension of belief is crucial. How to drive a woman mad other than by refusing to believe her? This is what George Cukor masterfully demonstrated in his film *Gaslight* (1944). The words of Paula, played by Ingrid Bergman, keep arousing suspicion from Gregory, who manipulates his wife so that she doubts her own sanity. Paula has forgotten something once again, she has lost a precious object once again, once again she has misplaced what he has given her. Paula tries to tell her husband that she does not understand why the jewel he has offered her in memory of his mother has disappeared, and claims she was sure she had left it in her handbag. But he does not believe her. He first looks at her with an air of sadness and then of outright disapproval.

He does not believe her simply because after killing the great actress Alice Alquist, Gregory's plan is to drive her niece mad so as to inherit her aunt's jewel. But Paula is unaware of this, and she thinks she is loved. She put faith in this encounter a little too rapidly and it led her to give up singing and music. She submitted to Gregory when he expressed the desire to come back to London and live in the house where Paula's aunt had mysteriously been assassinated. She submitted to this man while feeling that something was beginning to change drastically in her. A kind of fear took hold of her. Trapped in this house where a woman was assassinated, she was somehow haunted by the dead woman. She no longer knew who she was. Was she Paula? Was she a woman losing her head? Was it the murder of her aunt which came back to haunt her and deprive her of her clear-headedness? Was she simply and purely becoming crazy and yielding to the situation?

There are no limits to the concessions Paula can make for Gregory. Consenting not to appear in the street anymore, turning down all invitations, running away from the neighbours, remaining locked up in the house, not seeing anyone any longer, shutting herself in her bedroom to collect herself, trying to forget that she has forgotten. The more Gregory puts the blame on Paula for her words, her acts, and her memory, the more unstable Paula becomes. She ends up yielding to the situation by parting with her relation to truth. She finally believes Gregory and has the feeling that she is on the edge of an abyss of madness. She is ready to submit to what he himself wants: lead her to consent to end her life in an asylum.

Until the day when a man who knew and admired Paula's aunt notices the young woman, as she is allowed by Gregory for the first and only time to go out. It is on the occasion of a concert given by a lady of London's high society that this man, Brian Cameron, a detective from Scotland Yard (played by Joseph Cotten), looks at her and thinks he recognizes her aunt whom he knew well. He stares at her and tries to decipher the enigma of what is happening before his eyes. Paula's face expresses first the joy of listening to music beside her husband, the joy of being outside at last, since she was invited by this lady who had made her aunt's acquaintance.

Then, all of a sudden, confusion can be read in her eyes. Her husband has just whispered something into her ear. Panic takes hold of her as she is rummaging through her bag and looks as if she couldn't find the object she is searching for. The sobs that rack her body disrupt the concert and Gregory, who has achieved his goals, makes her stand up and leave the concert. The detective from Scotland Yard sees that something is happening between Paula and this man, which endangers her life. He believes that without knowing.

Paula is on the verge of descending into madness while her husband disappears every night into the attic and makes her believe that she is plagued by hallucinations (lights are dimming and footsteps resonate in the attic). She almost "yields to the situation." Yet, by chance, she finds an object the existence of which had been denied by Gregory; it is a letter which he had concealed in a book and which she had read. This lucky coincidence enables her now to be certain of what she knew. She understands that the love she had believed in never existed. At the same time, she is saved from this folly. Just in time, just before she yields to the situation that Gregory imposes on her, she finds her bearings again. She knows that what she told him was true. Meeting the detective from Scotland Yard who believes her enables her then to find herself again. Paula's story illustrates how important belief is. To be believed is to be able to find a place where the trauma, albeit inarticulable, is not denied but located and acknowledged.

The dimension of belief when a subject ventures to say something about his or her trauma, is therefore of paramount importance. The fact of being believed has to do with an ethics regarding the relation to speech. Not being believed duplicates the unspeakable character of the trauma. This encounter with someone who believes you implies specific conditions of speech, conditions which protect speech from any judgement, conditions which make the advent of a truth possible, conditions which mean that to a subject's revelation something specific can be answered. In short, speaking about a sexual trauma can either have a devastating effect or, on the contrary, produce an effect of reparation, depending on how it is responded to. What is needed is an encounter with a being to whom one can speak about it, in conditions which cannot be the conditions of ordinary speech. Because what happened to me in this place is not identical to what happened to somebody else. Each body is connected to the way one is affected, a way characteristic of each subject, and which resonates with his or her secret history.

To the bad encounter of the trauma, it is therefore necessary to be able to respond, afterwards, by a good encounter with someone who believes you. But what does it mean to believe in what a being tries to say about his or her psychological and sexual trauma? To believe in the words of a being who tries to say what is happening to them is not only to ascertain the objective reality of what happened. It is much more. To believe, as Lacan put it, "is less than knowing, but perhaps more."[6] Because to believe is already to commit oneself and commit whoever speaks to us in their own words, in their own history, in the adventure which consists in deciphering the indelible trace.

To be believed is even more necessary when it is a question of saying something of a sexual trauma. The subject yields again something of himself or herself by speaking about it. He or she does not only reveal a concealed truth. They open a field and even re-open a field which had left them on the edge of a precipice. They speak, confronted to an impossibility to say which must not be intensified by the Other's outright dismissal. There lies the risk, this feeling of an absolute risk taken by whoever tries to say something of the traumatic trace, to read it without knowing. While he or she is trying to articulate he unspeakable of trauma, the subject draws nearer the abyss where he or she once disappeared. If he or she is unable to say it, isn't it because it never happened this way? Doesn't it mean that doubt can conceal what is left from the traumatic situation? Everything is becoming unreal because what has been encountered has not managed to enter the world of language. The moments of depersonalization which can follow a traumatic experience bear witness to this frontier which has been crossed, from the world of "consent" to the world of "yielding."

Cession

The experience which consists in saying what took place in the body, saying this "cession," demands that one should lean on a new pact, the pact which will be set up between the subject who speaks and the Other who believes him or her. Here, the one who speaks does not denounce. He or she does not speak to denounce or accuse. They try to retrieve and say what they have lost because what matters then for them is to try and prove what could not be proved and left an indelible trace.

"Forever marked," Lacan insists. It means that this mark about which one speaks is not erased, resists the wear and tear of time, stays as a "foreign body"[7] in one's flesh – to use Freud's and Breuer's words – and, on top of this, produces something like a repetition. The first time that marked the subject's flesh for life subsequently engenders a series, which does not mean that the subject re-lives exactly the same thing from the point of view of the reality of facts, but that the subject, at different strategic moments of his or her existence, experiences the return of what could not be ascertained. As a never-ending return of the same impossibility to say.

Fixity, the unspeakable character of the traumatic situation, an indelible mark. Let's say it again with Lacan: "what occurred is something that gives its true meaning to the subject's *yield* – it's literally a cession."[8] What is then this cession in the literal sense? This is where the distinction between "to yield" and "to consent" takes a new meaning altogether. Between cession and consent the difference is obvious. "*Cedere*" related to "*cadere*,"[9] means to fall, to drop. The cession which Lacan invites us to take literally has to do with the legal meaning of the term, which is a transfer of rights. The subject who yields to the traumatic situation relinquishes his or her right over their bodies. They have no more claims on their bodies. They fall as subjects abandoned by the Other, reduced to their bodies. The subject has been erased and has yielded before the superiority of the traumatic situation. No weapon enables him or her to face what they encounter. No right exists any longer. In a way they are abandoned by their own bodies which are no longer present to ensure that they are alive. Something of the "body's identity"[10] prior to the constitution of the subject is ravished and lost.

When I have lost my body, how can I find myself again? How can I find again this knot which was undone at the moment when I yielded to the situation? The scream expresses what the subject yields, a piece of himself or herself. It is the experience of helplessness. One cannot do anything against it. Nobody in that situation can protect me anymore. I have yielded something, and nothing will ever conjoin me to it again.

Notes

1 Cf. footnote 1 in previous chapter.
2 Jacques Lacan, *The Seminar of Jacques Lacan. Book X*, "Anxiety", Ed. J.-A. Miller, Transl. A. R. Price, Polity, Cambridge, 2014, p. 312.
3 Lacan, p. 312.
4 Lacan, p. 312.
5 Lacan, p. 312.
6 Jacques Lacan, "Presentation on Psychic Causality", in *Écrits. The First Complete Edition in English*, Transl. Bruce Fink, W.W. Norton & Co., London/New York, 2006, p. 134.
7 Sigmund Freud, Joseph Breuer, "On The Psychical Mechanism of Hysterical Phenomena: Preliminary Communication from Studies on Hysteria", in *The Standard Edition of the Complete Psychological Works of Sigmund Freud*, Transl. James Strachey, Vol. II, Vintage Classics, London, 2001, p. 9.
8 Jacques Lacan, Jacques Lacan, *The Seminar of Jacques Lacan. Book X*, "Anxiety", Ed. J.-A. Miller, Transl. A. R. Price, Polity, Cambridge, 2014, p. 312.
9 Alain Rey, *Dictionnaire historique de la langue française*, Le Robert, Paris, 2000, p. 410.
10 Lacan, p. 314.

Chapter 8

Severed Tongue

One day, I had a dream which took me by surprise and even shocked me a great deal. I could not see where this dream emanated from or what it meant, and even less what message it conveyed. It was a dream that said nothing and even dealt with the impossibility to say. Yet I had been in analysis for a few years, and I was used to paying attention to my dreams, to associating afterwards, to learning a lesson from them and drawing a thread to keep speaking. I loved saying something in analysis and besides I always found something to say. That time, I mentioned the dream to the analyst without being able to say anything about it. What was this dream which confronted me for the first time to the experience of the unsayable?

"I dream that I am on my way to the analyst, as is my wont. I lie down on the couch. The analyst leans over me and instead of listening to me asks me to open my mouth. My mouth is wide open, and he stares inside. He grabs pincers and severs bits of tongue. I let it happen, though I am slightly surprised by what he is doing. At the end of the dream, I find myself with bits of tongue in my hand. I am holding them in my right hand, and I can feel the strange texture of the peculiar flesh of the tongue. I wonder if I will still be able to speak and kiss, with my tongue cut out like this. I throw the bits of tongue into the dustbin, and I leave." End of the dream.

This dream which is not connected to my personal history but to my relation to what I can say and to what I cannot, I called it "the dream of the severed tongue." I couldn't make sense of this dream which, I assumed, showed me that I was parting with something, with a certain relation to speech: my love for truth, perhaps? I even thought that, in some respect, this dream signaled the end of my analysis. *Final cut.*[1] I left, having thrown away bits of tongue without any feeling of nostalgia. But the analyst pointed out something which surprised me: "to have one's tongue cut out is also not being able to say." What do you know! Why hadn't I thought about it before? Does it mean there is something I am unable to say, even though I feel that, since I started a long time ago to go, I have always been able to say what I have to tell him? This encounter with the impossibility to say ushered in a new sequence in my analytical experience which I will put aside for now. What I have retained from this is that the encounter with the severed tongue is a metaphor of the encounter with a silence at the core of speech.

DOI: 10.4324/9781003536956-8

The story of a sexual trauma is always the story of a silence. It is the story of a mouth that has been locked. The story of words cut short on the edge of the lips, the story of a tongue which has been severed. Being no longer able to say what happened is part of the effects of the bad encounter. It is also the signal, as I pointed out above, that there has been a "cession." It also signals that what happened occurred *without* my consent.

When I had this dream of the severed tongue, I did not know the story of *Tereus and Philomela* to which I am going to come back now. Yet, I had looked it up in fables, here and there, because this story of the severed tongue – which for me slightly resonated with Hans Christian Andersen's fairy tale *The Little Mermaid* – was reminiscent I thought, of Greek mythology. The most ancient sources of the myth of Philomela are to be found in Hesiod and Homer, then in the fifth century BC in Aeschylus and Sophocles. But the tale in its entirety can only be found in more recent Latin sources, mainly Ovid, in his *Metamorphoses*.[2] Here, I am referring to Ovid's version.

"Her speechless lips couldn't tell the truth"[3] of what happened.

Philomela's Scream

Through the narration of the rape of Philomela, the daughter of Pandion I, King of Athens, by her brother-in law, King Tereus of Thrace, Ovid leads us where the subject can no longer say anything. This rape, analysed with a great deal of finesse by Pascal Quignard in *L'Homme aux Trois Lettres*, is followed in Ovid's myth by an event which has to do with confiscated speech. After raping Philomela, Tereus excises her tongue. Ovid's myth narrates the story of the silence that follows sexual trauma.

"Her speechless lips couldn't tell the truth"[4] of what happened.

How will Philomela still be able to tell the truth of what happened? Now deprived of her tongue, she is voiceless. No articulated sound can come out of her mouth. What happened exactly? It is "up to a stone but hidden away in an ancient forest,"[5] that Tereus from Thrace, betraying his wife and the father of his wife, abuses Philomela. There, he crosses the unimaginable by violating the father's speech and his wife's trust with the same gesture. Tereus rapes his wife's sister.

His wife, whose name is Procne, has informed him of her dearest wish, which is to see her sister Philomela, from whom she was separated after her wedding and who has remained in Athens in the family mansion ever since. Tereus, who had noticed how beautiful Philomela was, travels to Athens and visits his father-in-law Pandion to carry out his mission, which is to bring his wife's dearest sister back home. Pandion consents to entrust his son-in-law with his second daughter, out of love for Procne, and so that the two sisters can meet again. His words are testament both to his anxiety at letting the only daughter he has left move away from him for this voyage, and to his request to Tereus: "I entrust Philomela to you. Her sisterly kindness/has won me over. The two of them wanted it, so did you./Tereus, I trust you, you're one of the family. Please, in the name/of the gods I implore you, watch over my child with a father's love,/and return her soon-she is the comfort and balm of my anxious old age-/as soon as you can."[6]

More than a request, Pandion's message to his son-in-law is a supplication.

In the name of good faith, Pandion hands over to him what he holds dearest, now that Philomela is the only child he has left. In the name of the value of speech, he consents to part with his daughter. "Watch over my child with a father's love," Pandion tells him. It is the laws of marriage, based on speech that lead him to agree on this pact with Tereus: "Protect her out of love for me, your father-in-law, the father of your wife."

These are the laws of speech and language, which nobody is supposed to ignore. These are the laws of promise. But good faith no longer holds when faced with the compulsion of the drive. Speech no longer includes a single pact of trust. Tereus wants to enjoy this body, the body of his wife's sister. He is certainly no father, just a rapist. By acting this way, he knows that in Philomela he also targets her bond of sorority. He forces her to betray her sister. Human beings are not these gentle, good-natured people moved by love of the neigbour, but people who can be tempted to use sexually the body of another being without their consent, to make them suffer and even to kill them, as Freud remarked. Tereus is not a human being moved by love of the neighbour. He is not a gentle good-natured person. He is a tyrant whose behaviour is dictated by the demand of jouissance of Philomela's body. No promise holds any longer. The pact of speech does not function as a stopping point for what imposes itself to Tereus. *Without* her consent, he carries the young woman away to a place where no one will be able to hear her scream.

The young woman does not understand immediately what is happening: Where is her sister? Where has he taken her? What is this trap? "White and shaking in abject terror, she tearfully asked him, 'Where is my sister?' But now she was trapped. His ugly intentions/were all too clear. His virgin prize was alone, and he brutally/ raped her. Helpless she screamed in vain for her father, she screamed/for her sister and called above all on the gods to come to her rescue."[7] The rape takes place in this barn. That Philomela should call on another who could save her is also part of his jouissance.

Nobody can hear Philomela's screams. She may scream again and again. Nobody will save her from the hands of Tereus. There are no more gods to save her. In the twentieth century, Freud might have called it an experience of *Hilflösigkeit*. Terrified, trembling "like a frightened lamb,"[8] Philomela yields to the situation. Distressed, flustered, overwhelmed by a dreadful solitude in front of the other's drive: "what about me?" forgotten by all, finding herself where nobody can hear her screams, she is reduced to being nothing but a body that the other enjoys without her consent.

Not Keeping Quiet about What One Cannot Say

But once the rape has occurred, Philomela collects herself. Philomela finds words again while rejecting the body which Tereus enjoyed, her own: "she tore her dishevelled/hair, she scored her arms with her nails like a woman in grief/and cried with her arms outstretched,"[9] she curses Tereus: "You cruel barbarian! How could you/do such a dreadful deed? Were you wholly unmoved by my father's/entreaties and tears of devotion, my sister's longing to see me/respect for my maiden virtue and what you owed to your wife? Nature is overthrown!"[10]

Philomela wishes he had taken her life, now that her body has yielded, now that he has taken her body as if he were allowed to. However, Philomela, who is still alive, now wants to make Tereus atone for his crime. After the terror, the awe, and the trembling, after the stupefaction and the pain, she now experiences anger.

Philomela won't keep silent about this crime. She will speak and even scream to the whole world what Tereus has done in the barn. "I'll tell the world of your crime myself. If I'm given the chance, I'll cry it aloud in the marketplace, and if you still hold me/prisoner deep in the forest, my words will ring through the trees;/the rocks will know and be moved to pity by what I have suffered;/the sky will listen and so will the gods, if any exist there."[11]

Through her words, Philomela recovers something of what she has lost. She screams for revenge and this scream will be of the order of a saying. She will cross the barrier of modesty and will denounce this revolting crime. She will not be ashamed in his place. She will make her act public and destroy Tereus's reputation. Her voice will reverberate, and she will know how to move the cosmos that Tereus tarnished with his cruel act. She will bring shame upon him.

But Philomela's words unleash the anger of Tereus who is not yet done with the sexual use of this body.

"Her tongue was still voicing her sense of outrage and crying her father's name, still struggling to speak, when Tereus gripped it in pincers/and hacked it out with his sword. As its roots in her throat gave a flicker, the rest of it muttered and twitched where it dropped on the blood-black earth (…) Even after this crime, though the story is scarcely believable, Tereus debauched that bleeding body again and again."[12]

Absolutization of the jouissance of a woman's body, to the point of maiming this body, forcing it to keep silent, depriving it from the means to say that she is here. Tereus's fury now knows no limit. It is not only the pact he made with his father-in-law which is here violated, but also the relation to another human being's body, which suddenly falls into a limitless unleashing of the drive. It is the respect one owes to the living body which is abolished. It is the death drive which combines with the sexual drive to silence the one who, through her speech, throws back at him the meaning of the crime he commits, of the laws he flouts, of the very civilization he destroys. To enjoy her even more, he needs to silence her. For as long as she speaks, something of her own being is still slipping out of his control. She must be deprived of the means to arouse his shame by screaming her anger and her wish to take her revenge. She must have her tongue cut out.

The image of this piece of tongue darkened by blood and wailing to the earth is a sign that all possibility of address to the other disappears in the experience of subjective cession. This image of the severed tongue is a metaphor of the piece of body which has been torn off by the sexual trauma. It does not mean that the subject wavers or flags as Lacan puts it. It means that it falls, like this piece of tongue thrown onto the ground. What is left of Philomela's scream, what is left of her "no" is this torn off tongue, twitching and trembling, which has lost its body. I have lost my body.

"Her speechless lips couldn't tell the truth"[13] of what happened.

Philomela has been silenced. She has lost the ability to say. Will the pain remain forever silent? How would you say what has become impossible to say?

What can no longer be spoken must not be kept silent for all that. Philomela cannot continue to exist without saying. She must devise a means whereby she will let people know. She must inscribe this crime in the field of discourse. She must invent another language. It may not be a language that can be heard but at least it will be a language that shows what can be said no more. "But suffering sharpens the wits, and misfortune makes one resourceful. She craftily strung a warp on a primitive Thracian loom, and into the pure white threads she wove a message in purple/letters revealing the crime."[14] Immured, reduced to silence, Philomela finds a way to commemorate her trauma by weaving a narrative with a red thread onto a white background fabric.

It is by weaving the scene which depicts her trauma that she will give it a place in the world of the other. She allows one to read a wordless story on an embroidery. The image of the rape embroidered with red thread is a substitute for silence. Where she can no longer make her voice heard, Philomela makes the others see. She shows what happened to those who will be able to face up to the crime. The embroidery, handed over to a servant, will be entrusted to her sister. Procne will then carry out the worst act of vengeance, throwing back in Tereus's face, the horror of his crime.

From this myth, Pascal Quignard draws a lesson regarding what literature means as a practice of writing. "Literature is the true life, which narrates and gathers together the life that is fragmented, held back, confused, violated, wailing."[15] Literature is Philomela's silent song whose meaning must consequently be surmised on the web she has woven; it is the reading of these letters which have been confiscated by the world. Hers is a violated life turned into a story which must be deciphered, an image which must be interpreted and secret letters which must be found again.

This myth by Ovid also teaches us a lesson about sexual trauma, speech, and silence. I am here coming back to this appalling image with its extremely accurate metaphor: an excised tongue. Trauma is about a dead tongue. It deals with the silence surrounding what happened. It deals with a "not being able to speak about it" as if the encounter with the traumatic real had cut out my tongue.

How would we say then, in a living language, what precisely had the effect of cutting out my tongue, depriving me of my voice, preventing me from speaking out? Wasn't it this question that my dream was asking me? The unconscious sometimes precedes the dreamer and shows him or her what they are still unable to say themselves.

I cannot articulate what I ceded when I "yielded to" the situation.

Notes

1 In English in the original. [TN]
2 I refer here to Timothy Gantz's book, *Early Greek Myth: A Guide to Literary and Artistic Sources*, John Hopkins University Press, Baltimore, 1993.
3 Ovid, *Metamorphoses*, Transl. David Raeburn, Penguin Classics, 2004, p. 238.
4 Ovid, p. 238.
5 Ovid, p. 235.
6 Ovid, p. 234.
7 Ovid, p. 235.
8 Ovid, p. 235.
9 Ovid, p .236.
10 Ovid, p. 236.
11 Ovid, p. 236.
12 Ovid, p. 237.
13 Ovid, p. 235.
14 Ovidp. 238.
15 Pascal Quignard, *L'Homme aux trois lettres,* Grasset, Paris, 2020, p. 41.

Chapter 9

Who Will Believe Me?

I would now like to look deeper into this effect caused by sexual trauma, that of silencing people.

Following what happened, I would sometimes wish I could forget. Not think about it any longer and obliterate what cannot be obliterated. Why should I talk about it after all? To whom? "I wish to be wordless,"[1] Confucius wrote. Can silence be a remedy? Psychoanalysis bets on speech. You can say something about what is unsayable. Saying nothing is not to obliterate the event and treat it as if it never occurred. Saying nothing is also to remain haunted by the trauma.

But am I sure that my words will accurately and faithfully express what I cannot see clearly? I can already feel that whatever words one uses to speak about what happened, the realness of the event will be distorted. What occurred seems disjointed from the world of speech. The question of silence about the trauma endured and the difficulty to articulate was already pinpointed by Freud. Emma's silence at eight recurs when she is thirteen. It is because she breaks this silence by entrusting Freud with her symptom – being unable to enter a shop by herself – that she can retrieve the most recent memory which leads her then to the core of the trauma. The first memory, the traumatic event proper, bears the hallmark of silence. Only by consenting to the free association of ideas, starting off with the second memory, when she is 13, is she driven to that old place. The speechless scene which took place when she was eight, the scene where she could not understand what was happening, where she couldn't make sense of anything, the scene that was an effraction in her childhood, when her body became the object of jouissance of somebody she trusted. Because when you are an eight-year-old little girl, you trust the grocer who sells you sweets.

Hysterical neurosis prompted Freud to explore this silence, which he also called amnesia. The subject has forgotten. The mark of the trauma also resides in this memory lapse. Lacan goes as far as making of this lapse the very definition of the subject: "he can forget."[2] This is also the paradox of the indelible mark of trauma. It is always active, but the subject has forgotten it, can't recall it, in other words, they can't say it. Subjective cession concerns this subject. A threshold has been crossed that was not meant to be crossed. The turmoil experienced in the subject's body made them lose their composure. They have lost themselves. That they should

DOI: 10.4324/9781003536956-9

have forgotten what deeply affects them is of significance. They have forgotten what happened to them and yet they yielded to the traumatic situation which has rendered them wordless.

Dora's Sealed Lips

This is also what happened to Dora. When she was 14, the husband of a dear friend of her father's took advantage of his being alone with her to hold her tightly against him and kiss her on the mouth. "Dora had at that moment a violent feeling of disgust, tore herself free from the man and hurried past him to the staircase and from there to the street door."[3] Dora kept this scene secret as if she was both ashamed of him and ashamed of herself. Yet, as she continued to meet the K.'s – who were very close to her father – she also played a role in the clandestine relationship that formed between Mr. K. and her father.

A few years later, when Dora was eighteen, Mr. K declared his love for her. They were walking together along the lake, and he broke the silence: "you know I get nothing out of my wife."[4] Dora, who had not replied when she was fourteen, this time, at eighteen, slapped him in the face. Once again, she fell silent. But the slap was a "no" addressed to the one who had forced her when she was fourteen. The eighteen-year-old Dora may have welcomed this declaration of love differently, had it not brought up the memory of this first scene, when he forced her.

Here again, a double temporality is at play. The answer she was unable to articulate the first time still cannot be said. The slap is not an enunciation but an act which short-circuits her anxiety. Or rather the anxiety experienced in the body causes her to slap him in the face. Nevertheless, it is the answer "après coup" to the first trauma, four years later. It is the answer which did not occur the first time.

Why didn't Dora say a word during these four years? The scene by the lake had to take place for her to dare say something. In other words, Mr. K. had to utter what he expected from her and what his situation with his wife was, for Dora to let the event enter the speaking world. Dora no longer knew what place she should give the secret she had kept, the secret of what Mr. K. took away from her when she was fourteen. On this event her lips remained sealed. Yet she decided to denounce him. But she could not speak of the scene which occurred when she was fourteen, she could only speak of the scene which occurred when she was eighteen. She disclosed what happened by the lake to her mother and father.

Was she right to mention it? Did it help her to better know what she wanted, trapped as she was between the couples that were forming and those that were coming apart? Something she had not anticipated occurred then: nobody believed her. Though she confessed to her mother and father that Mr. K. made advances to her, she was disowned by all.

What, in Vienna of 1899, is a young eighteen-year-old girl's speech worth, compared to that of a distinguished man, married and father of two children? Instead of believing in his daughter's speech, in her own truth, her father wanted to check what she had said. He asked Mr. K. for explanations. The latter "denied in the most emphatic terms having on his side made any advances which could have been open to such a construction. He had then proceeded to throw suspicion upon the girl."[5] Considered as a compulsive liar, even by Mrs. K. who had become her own confidant, Dora found herself caught in the trap of her own words. The truth she wanted to impart to others turned against her. Breaking the silence, she found herself excluded from the world of the other, from this little world in which she had so far found a place: between her father and her mother, between her father and Mrs. K., between Mr. K. and Mrs. K., she no longer knew what she was seeking among them.

If nobody wanted to believe her, what was the point of carrying on living? Following the liberation of her speech and after facing such a disavowal, Dora left a farewell letter to her parents announcing her desire to take her own life. Her parents came across the letter which she had left in her writing-desk, and they panicked. They understood that their daughter needed help. Anxious to help his daughter, the father took her to see Freud.

What is noteworthy here is that he speaks to Freud about his daughter, casting doubt on her speech: "I myself believe that Dora's tale of the man's immoral suggestions is a phantasy that has forced its way into her mind,"[6] he says. A phantasy that has forced its way into her mind? Almost driving her mad, as Gregory did with Paula, Dora's father has notwithstanding the intuition that somebody must believe her. If he can't, trapped in his will not to break up with the K.'s in order to continue his affair with Mrs. K., then may be Freud can. In truth, Freud is not fooled by the father's words and, before anything else, takes an interest in what Dora is trying to tell him about the crisis she is going through. When Dora introduces herself to Freud, her symptom is aphonia. She has lost her voice. Like Philomela whose tongue was severed, like the Little Mermaid who can no longer say who she is, Dora is deprived of the means to speak about herself. As if under a strange evil spell, not only does the sexual and psychological trauma assaults the subject, but it also condemns him or her to the impossibility to say. Dora remains silent on her suffering. The traumatic event to which she yielded without consenting is eventually allowed to be articulated, for the first time, somewhere, in this office situated 19 Berggasse Street, where Freud listens to her. Never before did she tell anyone what had happened during the religious procession, where she found herself alone in the store with Mr. K. who clasped her to him and forcefully kissed her.

The Residue of Trauma, Untranslatable

Meeting an Other who believes them is a landmark in the life of a subject. It is an event which can change everything. Because at last, a door opens into a place where nobody judges if what you say conforms to reality; here you are welcomed from the truth of the words you attempt to articulate, the truth of what happened to you, and to you only. This speech is to be distinguished from the one which takes place during a trial. The purpose is not to accuse but to acknowledge the truth of the subject and the real of the body. What matters is that he or she attempts to articulate something of what first emerged in silence, as something which cannot be articulated.

But to break this silence, which has so far been maintained like a gag on the subject's speech, one needs to encounter a specific response. Otherwise, it is very likely that my words will be discredited by the Other, either because of the anxiety it may arouse in them or because it will be flatly denied. Treated with skepticism, regarded as exaggerated, even imaginary, the words then backfire onto the subject. The trauma somehow becomes redoubled. For speech about this indelible mark to have value, the truth about what I am saying must be acknowledged, even though I find a limit to what I can say, even though I fail to tell the whole truth, even though I realize that there is something which is impossible to say. There lies the whole challenge of speech about sexual and psychological trauma.

The value of my speech must be ascertained by another capable of making that speech resonate with silence. In other words, beyond what I attempt to say about the traumatic situation, there is also all that my words echo without being able to say it. This is where I find myself when it comes to expressing what is unspeakable in trauma: in this territory where it is as much a question of saying as of making silence resonate. What occurred cannot be wholly translated by words, nevertheless, through what they are saying, words can echo what they fail to say, and which is truly real. This zone of the "real" led Lacan to use the term "half-said," which points to this impossibility to tell the whole truth about trauma. The encounter with a severed tongue does not suggest the "non-existence" of trauma but, on the contrary, the real dimension of a trauma which has upset my relationship to speech to such a degree, that it is in this locus of speech that I experience the effects of trauma.

It is because this mark, which is both indelible and unreadable, fails to reveal itself in the first place, namely, to be brought to light and be acknowledged, for the subject and by them, that it leaves traces-echoes of the trauma without being the trauma itself. First, there is this indelible mark, then these traces that one tracks, these remnants of the indelible mark which one encounters and attempts to read by speaking about what fails to reveal itself. Speaking about trauma is then to confront oneself to this knot of *untranslatability*. It is to attempt through words to "make a trace of what has failed to establish itself from the start,"[7] to use Lacan's terms. Because what happened first caused an earth-shaking reaction in the subject's body. What remains is a hole. How to articulate what no longer relates to words but what hit one's body?

Psychoanalysis as an experience of speech confronts the subject with another dimension of speech, different from the one which concerns the recognition of the truth of what is said. It leads one to face the inability to say exactly what this trauma is. Yet, while experiencing its inadequacy, speech can draw closer to the core of the trauma. Lacan's premise is that the subject has been confronted to such a cession that, each time they find themselves at the crossroads of speech, the real that has left a mark on them is avoided. The subject endeavours to say it, but never quite succeeds completely. Not because of a failure inherent in speech but because of the very nature of this indelible mark which broke into the world of speech. This mark is then commemorated through repetition and the impossibility to fully articulate it. The mark left by the sexual and psychological trauma can be read little by little in the course of the analysis, as a black hole without meaning, except that it shows, where meaning is absent, the indelible character of the traumatic event.

This is what came back to me, from the dream of the severed tongue. After exploring the region of the truth of my story, it is to the region of the real that I intended to venture into when the dream of the severed tongue occurred. This is what the dream was showing me without being able to say it. Yes, you may continue to speak but your speech will no longer lean on your love for truth. Your speech will become a foreign language, as if you had to learn a new language, the moment the one you were familiar with can no longer teach you anything new.

What one cannot articulate, one must not keep silent.

What I had to cede, I must attempt to say it all the same.

Tereus' unleashing of the sexual drive when faced with Philomela illustrates the devastating effect of the encounter with the real for the subject. Traumas have consequences on the body and on speech. Whether it be sexual trauma, war trauma or psychological trauma. The tragic aspect lies in the experience of the severed tongue which bears witness to the impossibility to say what remains from the event. Yet, facing the unsayable means that one should nonetheless invent something: like Philomela with her embroidery, like Emma with her obsessive fear of not being able to enter a store alone, like Dora with her aphonia and her desire to speak to Freud. One must invent a language of one's own, to echo Virginia Woolf's "room of one's own." Venturing into this territory of the real is to spell the letters of a new alphabet, the words of an unknown language which I can speak without knowing it, to articulate what affected me in my flesh. The new living language the subject must invent is what psychoanalysis, but also art, and in particular literature, are about. A language I can speak from the most intimate part of my being, the part that encountered a dimension of the real which has left me speechless.

Notes

1 Confucius, *The Analects of Confucius*, R. Eno, 2015, p. 98.
2 Jacques Lacan, "The Ethics of Psychoanalysis", in *The Seminar of Jacques Lacan, Book VII*, Ed. J.-A Miller, Transl. Dennis Porter, W.W. Norton & Co, New York/London, 1992, p. 264.
3 Sigmund Freud, "Fragments of an Analysis of a Case of Hysteria", in *The Complete Psychological Works of Sigmund Freud*, Transl. James Strachey, Vol. VII, Vintage Classics, New York, 2001, p. 28.
4 Freud, p. 98.
5 Freud, p. 26.
6 Freud, p. 26.
7 Jacques Lacan, "Radiophonie", in *Autres Écrits*, Seuil, Paris, 2001, p. 428.

Chapter 10

Reviving Silence, Coming Back from It

The silence that had reigned during the war and for a short while afterward seemed to be swallowed up in an ocean of words. The really huge catastrophes are the ones that we tend to surround with words so as to protect ourselves from them. The first words that I wrote were a kind of desperate cry to find the silence that had enfolded me during the war. A sixth sense told me that my soul was enveloped in this same silence and that if I managed to revive it, the right words would come.[1]

How is it possible to speak again after a traumatic encounter, when I was deprived of the possibility to utter a word because of a severed tongue? Is it not necessary to come back to a form of silence from which new words may resonate, words that are different from ordinary speech, and which would truly belong to the subjective cession I have gone through?

Reviving silence trough writing, such is the way chosen by writer Aharon Appelfeld to try to recover what took place in his body, when he was a ten-year-old child during the Second World War. Trauma will always rouse distress for the child who finds himself utterly defenseless, dejection for the human being who calls for help but whose request is not heard and loneliness for the one whose questions remain unanswered. In *The Story of a Life*, Aharon Appelfeld revives the silence of the war trauma he experienced when he was only a child.

When a singular trauma, the trauma which a human being experiences in the intimacy of their existence, encounters a historical "collective" trauma such as the Second World War for instance, the question is to know how it will be possible to find a singular way of speaking about what happened to me. The words used by others about a historical catastrophe, "the ocean of words," as Ahron Appelfeld put it, may have a paradoxical retroactive effect: while the event is acknowledged in its historical reality, at the same time, the singular effect of the event on my body is disregarded or left out of consideration. It is as if too many words, noisy speeches, and the massive generalizing of too many interpretations ended up silencing the singular experience of each, as if the "WE" kept the "I" silent. This is where the testimony pronounced in the first-person singular takes on a new value. To find out how to write about what he went through as a child during the Second World War,

DOI: 10.4324/9781003536956-10

alone in the Ukrainian forests, after surviving the death of his parents in a concentration camp, Appelfeld contends that it is necessary to revive silence. As if at one point, retroactively, in the "après-coup" of the trauma, words acquired a value only if snatched away from silence. As if being silent made it possible to recover part of the traumatic trace in its least communicable yet most real aspect. When the ocean of words come from the others, it also has the effect of robbing the subject of his or her own words. The difficulty, as he writes in *The Story of a Life*, was for Aharon Appelfeld to "safeguard that core of myself that was being asked to be something it didn't want to be and could not be."[2] "We" have never experienced the "same" thing, although the trauma of Nazism is part of the history of the people who had to endure its destructive effects. Each human being was affected in a way that only he or she can make real, through a testimony, a word, a written text, a piece of work.

The question here centres on the necessity to reconnect with the country of words starting from an event which produced an effraction in the world of words and in someone's life.

Added to the bodily effraction, sexual trauma or war trauma always includes a psychical shock which is silent: how then can one speak again when speech has been silenced? "For many years, I was plunged in an amnesiac slumber. My life was going by on the surface. I had grown accustomed to buried and damp cellars."[3]

Within this study which has been a clinical and political but also philosophical and literary analysis oriented by the aphorism: "to yield is not to consent," I am now reaching the core of the silence that lies at the heart of the subjective cession. It is there that being silent sometimes becomes necessary to be able to say, without the *ocean of words*, the chatter of our ordinary discourse, the steady flow of ceaseless conversations, covering up the indelible mark of trauma.

Yielding to the Terror of War

After exploring the effects of sexual traumas, Freud began in 1920 to tackle another side of trauma, the trauma that stems from the catastrophe of war. One could argue that war trauma is for soldiers what sexual trauma is for Freud's first patients who suffered from hysterical symptoms.

The assertion "yielding is not consenting" is as true for war trauma as it is for sexual trauma. I could start by differentiating between the soldier who consents and believes in his fight and the soldier who is forced to go into battle even though he does not believe in it. It begins with forcing the soldier into battle without their consent, and without their fully comprehending the war. But this is not enough to account for the war trauma. This trauma is intensified by the encounter with a barbaric situation which causes a subjective cession. The soldier may force himself to comply orders without really believing in them. But the turning-point occurs when he is exposed to a concrete shock which has the same effect on the psyche as an explosion. This subjective cession may also occur with the consenting soldier who believes in the war he is waging and yet is not ready to encounter what war forces him to experience.

There, too, the distinction between "to yield" and "to consent" is crucial. That the soldier comes back from the battlefield not only with an injury but also with a psychological trauma, shows that the event for which he could not be prepared broke into the body. War trauma makes the frontier between "yielding" and "consenting" visible. One could argue that whatever the subjective involvement of a soldier in the war he participates in, this involvement does not mean that the soldier is ready. This is what Stanley Kubrick showed in his film about the Vietnam war. Whatever the soldiers' preparation, however strict and violent it may be, they will never be protected from what they will have to live through. They will never be ready.

Divided into two parts, *Full Metal Jacket* (1987) exposes this yawning gap. Between the soldiers' preparation which takes up the first part of the film and the arrival in the field, in Vietnam (the second part), there is no relation whatsoever. Nothing can equip the soldiers against the real of war. War is always a confrontation with a situation which will produce an effraction into the subject's psyche. That is why, in this case, the soldier who consents – if it is the case – is confronted to something totally different from what he had expected.

The encounter with war trauma lays bare what a subjective cession is. How does one account for the nightmare which awakens the soldier, confronting him with the repetition of the horror he has lived through? How does one explain that the subject relives through his nightmares the trauma of war? The psychological effects of the war on the soldiers back from the battleground, led Freud to reconsider his theory of dreams as wish-fulfilment. The psychological world of the traumatized dreamer has become anxiety-inducing and has no longer anything to do with the fulfilment of a wish. Trauma has affected the core of the psyche, reverberating on the function of the dream. It is not only the conscious man who is awake and feels the effects of the traumatic situation; it is also the dreamer whose unconscious does not manage to fulfil itself in a dream. The subject incapable of dreaming again or even sleeping – the dream no longer fulfilling its function as a "guardian of sleep" – is confronted to the enigmatic return of the traumatic scene in the middle of the night. What he could not say, what he was unable to respond to, what he had to yield to, comes back to him through his nightmare. So, he wakes up, feeling the return of the terror he felt the first time he yielded to the situation.

The signs of traumatic neurosis, Freud writes, bear the mark of an intense subjective suffering, more acute than the signs of hysterical neurosis which he first encountered as he was venturing into the discovery of the unconscious. Freud distinguishes three affects relative to war trauma: fright, fear and anxiety [*Angst*]. Since Kierkegaard up to Sartre by way of Heidegger, the distinction between fear and anxiety has been central in existentialist philosophy. Fear is fear in front of an known object, a phenomenon taking place in the world. In short, when I am afraid, I know what I am afraid of: "'fear' requires a definite object of which to be afraid."[4] Freud's clinical observation is evocative of existentialism. Fear has an object. Anxiety, however, as Freud shows, can only be observed through clinical study. Anxiety is not anxiety in front of the void, existence or freedom. Anxiety according to Freud is an effect of the body which signals a danger.

"'Anxiety' describes a particular state of expecting the danger or preparing for it, even though it may be an unknown one."[5] Freud considers anxiety as the signal in the body of a danger to come. In that respect, anxiety protects the subject. If the subject has not sensed the danger, he or she can nevertheless lean on the anxiety which they experience to get ready for an event that could threaten them or make them run a risk, vital and drive-related. Anxiety precedes danger by anticipating it in the body.

The subject is somehow lucky to experience a feeling of anxiety before encountering the situation which puts them in danger. The anxious subject senses that something may happen to them, and they can already protect themselves from it even though this something remains unknown to them. Anxiety is thus at play when the signal of the danger emerges in the body as an affect which foreshadows future developments, without the subject being able to identify an object making them anxious. Fear is at play when one encounters a situation connected to a danger in the outside world. When I am afraid, I can run away from this danger. When I feel anxiety, I cannot run away because I don't know what is going to happen. However, I am prepared for it. Lacan pointed out that anxiety is not without object, which means that something does induce anxiety in me but that this thing cannot be identified as an object in the world, as in the case of fear. It is there but I don't know where. It could even be in my body. It could even identify with this signal, which sometimes causes me, beyond anxiety, to panic or overreact.

But what are the effects of a danger one encounters "without" being prepared for it? What happens then, in this body which has so far been mine, when the traumatic situation bursts in while nothing helped me to be prepared for it, to defend and protect myself against it, to seek refuge elsewhere. The affect which Freud points to is fright. The experience of subjective cession in the trauma is not associated with anxiety or fear, but with fright, terror. And when fright emerges, it is already too late. According to Freud, fright "is the name we give to the state a person experiences when he has run into danger without being prepared for it."[6] Fright is always linked to this absence of preparation. There, "yielding" will make its way through by short-circuiting the time of anxiety which could not take place.

"I do not believe anxiety can produce a traumatic neurosis. There is something about anxiety that protects its subject against fright and so against fright-neuroses."[7] The subject is surprised by a danger that forces itself upon him or her without any expectation of this danger preceding the event. Not only was nothing said but nothing was sensed or felt in the body either. The subject is trapped and his sensitivity to the other's words, voice, gaze and gestures has been assaulted.

Something suddenly cracked, shook the earth under my feet as if I had fallen into a bottomless hole. It was too strong, too intense, too loud, too violent. It was not for me and yet I was there, and I found myself without a self, robbed of my voice, howling my distress or silencing my terror.

The aphorism "yielding is not consenting" can thus be understood from the point of view of the subject who yields to a situation where he encounters fright. Trauma is in fact a journey to hell as well as a compulsion to repeat which can't be accounted for from the logic of conscience or reason. There lies the mystery. Why does the traumatic experience return in the nightmares of the soldiers who are back from the battlefield? Freud discovers that the psyche itself can be hit by what happened in the body, thereby short-circuiting anxiety: "dreams occurring in traumatic neuroses have the characteristic of repeatedly bringing the patient back into the situation of his accident, a situation from which he wakes up in another fright."[8] This is where the effect of the trauma lies. It is this return. The never-ending return which nobody can possibly call for and which yet imposes itself in a nightmare recurring again and again.

This is the nightmare of trauma: the initial experience seems to recur endlessly. As if what has not been grasped the first time, what has produced an explosion in the body without the subject being in the least prepared to it, what has emerged as a frightful surprise, came back unrelentingly to write a message which cannot be written. Because what happened does not enter the world of words, it fractures it.

War trauma teaches Freud that not only does the traumatic event leave a mark which does not suffer the wear and tear of time and seems indelible, something he had observed in psychological and sexual traumas, but it also tends to recur ceaselessly in the subject's psychical life. This is what he calls the manifestation of a repetition compulsion, which can also be called the destiny of a subject, in so far as this destiny is that which was written for him, from his singular trauma. To sum up, the traumatic event shattered the frame of space and time. It can no more be comprehended through ordinary sensitive experience. It occurred without the subject being able to perceive and comprehend it through sensitivity and thought. It forced itself upon him, shaking the very structure within which psychical life unfolds. It pierced the land of words and cast a shadow over the world.

Nick's Journey to Hell

What happened to Nick and why doesn't he come back home once the war is over? Nick will never return home because he can no longer go back. Nick yielded to a traumatic situation which condemned him to a diabolical repetition. Such is his journey to hell.[9] The scene took place while he and his comrades were prisoners in the jungle and compelled by their jailer to play Russian roulette. In twos, they confront each prisoner to this game, by betting on the one who will be struck in the head by the bullet. One bullet in the revolver and two men who are playing. After a few rounds, the bullet eventually kills the companion he is facing, before his very eyes. One is bound to die while the other will stay alive.

It is Mike's turn first. He (Robert De Niro) is forced to play with Steve (John Savage). They play, and Steve manages to divert the bullet which was about to go through his skull. The jailers keep betting. Mike, who has come back into the bamboo cage, has had the time to see and count: he needs three bullets to kill them, three bullets he will have to play by increasing the risk of dying, for both; but he will have to bet on Kairos to catch the torturers unaware. Now it's Nick's (Christopher Walken) turn. Mike must play with him next. He has informed him about his plan and Nick already takes fright. Three bullets instead of one. Nick hangs onto Mike's gaze, hangs onto his words, his voice, to shake off the fright and be able to play as Mike orders him to do. Nick can feel that he won't manage, that he can't face this situation. As for Mike, he is prepared for it. Robert de Niro embodies the heroic position of one who has overcome the barrier of death and who can face the situation without yielding to fright.

Three is the number of bullets he needs to consent to play, this is what he asks for to the torturers. For the jailers it makes no sense, but they arrange to grant him three bullets. They laugh and so does Mike, as if he was seized with a mad desire to die, possessed by this game of life and death. Nick consents because he has no choice. He also consents because he trusts Mike, but his body says "no." Each time he squeezes the trigger aimed at his temple, he strains the limits of his body. The incredible aspect of this scene in Michael Cimino's film, is to plunge as far as possible into this moment when consent gives rise to subjective cession.

The scene between Nick and Mike playing Russian roulette under the screams of their jailers is unprecedented in the history of cinema. The look in Mike's eyes, when he yields to the situation is unparalleled. Mike asks him to do exactly as he is told. To play a game of Russian roulette by aiming his weapon against his temple, with the three bullets in his gun, and to concentrate on his gaze and voice only. Nick wants to forget that he is afraid of dying, he wants to trust Mike's words even if fright has already taken hold of him. He wants to consent to trust him. But in doing so, he crosses the limit of the feeling of life. He forces himself to do away with what he feels as a living being to follow what Mike says.

For Mike to take action by catching the jailers unaware, Nick must shoot once. He must take the risk because only on this condition will the jailers be surprised too, and only then will he have an opportunity to kill them while they are not expecting it. What does it mean at this moment that Nick yields to the situation? It literally means that he forces himself to pull the trigger at his temple as if he consented to kill himself by playing in front of the others.

This scene, which is perhaps one of the most gruesome scenes ever filmed, powerfully shows the experience of trauma as psychical trauma. Nick doesn't manage to shoot at himself. He yields under the effects of the jailers' slaps. He hangs onto Mike's gaze. His existence now depends on what connects him to his friend's gaze. For Nick, shooting at his temple though he did not consent to it, means yielding to the situation and finally considering himself already dead.

It is Mike's turn to gamble on his life. Before he attacks the jailers, his face contorts into a strange smile as if overwhelmed by the exhilaration of the game. For a split second, while the jailers are staring at him in a daze, he deflects the bullet and shoots one of them, grabs the sub-machine gun, killing the other two. Mike has succeeded.

Nick can no longer be separated from Mike. He will no longer be able to find himself, to find his own body without Mike's body, without Mike's presence and gaze, from which he drew strength. Separated from Mike when an American helicopter rescues the soldiers from their hell, Nick screams.

Once the war is over, having lost Mike, Nick can't help gambling and playing Russian roulette. He will never be able to return. He will remain fixated on the traumatic scene, playing it again and again, not only in dreams but in real life. This is the nightmare that Freud describes as stemming from war neuroses. His life enacts, over and over again, the fright of losing it (this life) of his own accord. Because Nick's trauma is not only that he risked his life, but also that he had to pretend he was taking his life by his own hands. Nick's consent which was a "yes" to Mike, was crushed by the trauma. The forcing of his body undid the bond he had with life. Without Mike, he can no longer exist.

Nick will no longer leave Saigon. He won't experience anything except the scene of playing Russian roulette, re-enacting it repeatedly in Saigon's gambling dives. He will win money by gambling, because he is no longer afraid. Something of the relation to fear and anxiety has been crossed over forever. The fright was such that the only thing he could do was to repeat what caused him to disappear the first time. Through Nick's tragical destiny, Michael Cimino's *Deer Hunter* shows what the repetition compulsion means, and the hell it condemns the subject to.

The Narrative of the Trauma

Scraps of Discourse

Reviving silence means coming back from it.

It means coming back from it, but not by remaining fixated on the trauma, obsessed by the very places where it happened. After all there are two ways of going back: one which condemns the subject to repeat what happened and the other, which leads one to come back on one's own with words, discourse, writing. Coming back from it is to try and find with one's own language, that which is closest to the body and to the effects of the words on the body, a voice which will give rise to an account of the traumatic event. Sometimes writing can become the place where it is possible to say the unsayable of trauma. Sometimes solitude, silence, reuniting with a lost intimacy are the paths which enable one to recover speech. For some, this is the case of the artist Christian Boltanski, human heartbeats resonate at the heart of their works of art, so that below the words, the body can be heard fully alive. Others, like Philippe Lançon, find solace in the beauty of Bach's fugues played by the pianist Zhu Xiao-Mei, to reconnect with the sonority of the world. As if the relationship to the void was necessary to recapture the moment when one had one's breath taken away.

"I gradually started to read newspapers on the internet, and I was stunned by the amazing ability of the contemporary world to chat and provide explanations and commentaries about everything and anything."[10] Just like Aharon Appelfeld, Philippe Lançon writes about the necessity to revive a form of silence in order to come back from it. It takes time to release words that can speak about the trauma. The account of the trauma is more like a "scrap of discourse,"[11] to quote Lacan, than an ocean of commentaries. It is a fragment, a collection of scattered pieces, extracts of text full of holes, which are many attempts to give a place to what has been excluded from the world of words. The ocean of commentaries, the flood of analysis, the efforts to explain, and to give a meaning to what happened have veiled something at the same time. Philippe Lançon's writing was different from these discourses which in the end no longer dealt with the real of the trauma, having injected so many reasons, explanations, and meaning whilst what had suddenly burst through the life of the subject, had bereft the world of meaning.

Le Lambeau, published in 2018, is a narrative which at last recounted the traumatic event which took place in France in 2015.

The title chosen by Philippe Lançon borrows from the language of surgery, to express beyond the surgery of the wounded body, the surgery of the being himself. I will use Lacan's expression to designate the effect of the *Lambeau* (scrap): it acted as a *quilting point*. It stitched back up something that had opened up raw. The resurrection of silence sometimes goes through literature. The written text, accounts, fiction or testimonies, enable the subject to give birth to another language. The slowness of writing can be redeeming because the time necessary to say is not unconnected to the silence which imposed itself the first time, leaving the subject deprived of language. Reading is also a time when one tears oneself away from the humming and buzzing of discourses, immersing oneself in the voice of one person only.

While, since January 2015, speech, commentaries, media reports, and newspapers had relentlessly sought to make sense of what had happened, Philippe Lançon wrote – from 7 January up until the end of the year – without trying to find a meaning. His book silenced what he called the *abjection of thought*, referring to the will to immediately give a meaning to the event. By grasping what trauma is, the anxiety which emerges every evening in room 106, the madness that is "to be captive of the cruel and unthinkable event,"[12] the narrative somehow blocked up the hole which opened that year in France for each one. In that respect, it acted as a quilting point. Only a literary account, only an effort to write what remains impossible to say, could have this effect.

It is the particular effect literature has, that of being able to deal with an event which was a collective trauma, through the written language of one only.

Philippe Lançon's narrative teaches something about cession and its effects. It shows that it is no more a question of finding a meaning, of revealing a truth, but only of following the thread of the real. *Le Lambeau* recounts how a subject was able to return from the world of the dead, through writing. The writing of the real is precisely this, an effort to come back. Lançon recounts what, in Freud's words, cannot be assimilated. This is the term I haven't used so far. The unassimilable element of trauma imposes itself retroactively, after the event. What can be assimilated neither by the body nor by the world of words remains there, intact, threatening, shaking the foundations of being.

How then is it possible to retrieve speech? Philippe Lançon invents a trajectory: take up what occurred before, find the childhood events awakened by the bad encounter with the real, centre around what will forever remain indelible. One must draw near the *Monster of the mind*[13] with Bach's *Art of Fugue*, without being swallowed. The narrative of the real takes on the shape of a narrative of the body: of sensations, of vibrations. I will use Appelfeld's words in *The Story of a Life* to define what such book is: "This is not a book that asks questions and responds to them. These pages are a description of a struggle."[14]

This is perhaps what following the thread of the real means. The questions and answers can't stick to the real because they are too intent on discovering the truth. The thread of the real is not to be found easily, because it is not the thread of meaning. It is what happens in the body, shaking our relation to language.

With Philippe Lançon, following the thread of the real is writing about the hospital as a special place, a refuge, a shelter, a second skin which protects from the violence of the world. The hospital is not just a place of confinement but a closed world where he is able to return to life.

"These rooms had become my ports, my cabins."[15] In hospital, the relation to speech is as close as possible to the body being treated. Paradoxically, the traumatized body can express itself aptly in a language which itself would be traumatized by a totalitarian regime. "Big Brother's Newspeak in George Orwell's novel 1984 allowed me to formulate without saying it, what I felt in the first of my rooms: my floating state was that of a 'deadalive' and the reflex best suited to it was a 'yesno.'"[16]

There are also those who inhabit the hospital: Christian, the night nurse, whom he calls "Brother Morphine," Linda the nursing assistant, bright-eyed Annette, the nurse anaesthetist, and also Chloe, the surgeon in stomatology. The tie forged with the woman who gives him back a face is out of the ordinary, neither love nor friendship, but sheer trust. Chloe becomes the Other he can turn to. She what Freud called *Nebenmensch,* the Other on whom you can count. He has no other choice but to trust her words so that his body can come to life.

"Chloe, my surgeon, thinks I must leave the hospital quite soon now, to reconnect with life."[17] The scrap, a term she uses to name the autograft, is also the term that names the narrative about the real, a narrative which shows how a body is brought back to life through literature. There is indeed what is worth saying, and also what is worth writing and being read. Because listening, reading the solution of one alone, how he or she responds to the real, is to learn from them how I can in turn find my way to respond to my personal trauma.

The summer I finished reading *Le Lambeau*, I could not read another book. Something so strong had happened that it was impossible to read anything else afterwards. It took time to get used to the being who had found himself. Time to let Lançon's prose continue to live, before other words, other books, could follow.

Silence had to be revived.

Notes

1 Aharon Appelfeld, *The Story of a Life*, Transl. Aloma Halter, London, Penguin Books, 2004, p. 105.
2 Appelfeld, p. 116.
3 Appelfeld, p. 10.

4 Sigmund Freud, "Beyond the Pleasure Principle" (1920) in *The Standard Edition of the Complete Psychological Works of Sigmund Freud*, Transl. James Strachey, Vol. XVIII, Vintage Classics, London, 2001, p. 12.
5 Freud, p. 12.
6 Freud, p. 12.
7 Freud, pp. 12–13.
8 Freud, p. 13.
9 *Voyage au bout de l'enfer*, title in French of the film *Deer Hunter* by Michael Cimino. [TN]
10 Philippe Lançon, *Disturbance, Surviving Charle Hebdo* [*Le Lambeau*], Transl. Steven Randall, Europa Éditions, 2019, p. 274.
11 Jacques Lacan, "Psychoanalysis and Its Teaching", in *Écrits. The First Complete Edition in English*, Transl. Bruce Fink, W.W. Norton & Co., London/New York, 2006, p. 447.
12 Lacan, p. 209.
13 Philippe Lançon, "Les monstres de Bormazo", in *Ornicar*, n°53, 2020, p. 50.
14 Appelfeld, p. 8.
15 Appelfeld, p. 102.
16 Appelfeld, p. 100.
17 Appelfeld, p. 393.

Chapter 11

Consenting to Be Other to Oneself

After this journey to hell, after the resurrection of the silence, and the importance given to the first-person narrative about trauma, I would like to come back to love and to my starting point which was the enigma of consent. I want you by contrast, to breathe the air of consent, which is not that of subjective cession.

Why is consent, in the clinical sense of the term, so precious? What is this specific value of consent in particular in one's sexual and love life? Giving a psychoanalytical meaning to consent leads me to try to grasp what is opaque and contingent about consent. As I remarked from the outset, there is no consent that is wholly enlightened. It means that regarding sexual life, consent is not a kind of contract made with another to express a will or an agreement given in a free and enlightened way. In the field of love, such a definition of consent would empty the love experience from its value as well as its enigmatic power.

I now wish to propose a psychoanalytical approach to consent based on Lacan's groundbreaking contribution to feminine sexuality. Lacan gave a completely new meaning to the term femininity by conceiving it as a subjective and bodily experience and not as an anatomical determinism or a gender norm. According to him, it is a specific experience, which everyone, regardless of their anatomical sex, can experience, provided they lend themselves to it, consent to it, and provided they come across it at a certain moment in their lives.

Consent doesn't go without Kairos, the opportunity offered by chance to the subject, so that he or she may inscribe contingency at the heart of their lives. When one seizes an opportune moment, one acts without thinking and without knowing. One feels that it is a joyful chance which may have never happened and yet does happen. One can't wait for another moment to act. Consent to a chance encounter has to do with consent to femininity such as Lacan understood it. If consent is to let go of oneself, so is femininity, if consent is to "give in," so is femininity; if consent is a way to throw oneself into an adventure which makes us feel more alive, though we don't know all the ins and outs of it, so does femininity; if consent is a matter of intimate choice and bodily vibration, so is femininity. I am not alluding to femininity as a norm, a disguise, a role, but as a form of jouissance which Lacan called feminine, to give it a different status from that of masculine jouissance.

DOI: 10.4324/9781003536956-11

Consent to femininity is a kind of "yes," an opening to the Other, a surprise of desire, of love and jouissance. To take up Virginia Woolf's words, it is something like an unexpected discovery which touches the body. It is, for instance, what happens to Angela, when she opens her eyes onto the world. After "the dark churning of myriad ages here was light at the end of the tunnel; life; the world. Beneath her it lay – all good; all lovable. Such was her discovery. [...] She lay in this good world this new world, this world at the end of the tunnel, until a desire to see it or forestall it drove her, tossing her blankets, to guide herself towards the window, and there, looking out upon the garden, where the mist lay, all the windows open, one fiery-bluish, something murmuring in the distance, the world of course, and the morning coming, 'Oh,' she cried, as if in pain."[1]

Driven by the desire to go out to meet the world, Angela comes out of the tunnel. Feminine jouissance such as is understood by Lacan, evokes this "Oh" which comes out of Angela's mouth. It is an experience of "letting yourself be surprised" by desire as if by the morning coming.

Consenting to Split Oneself into Two

Feeling that you are a woman has nothing to do with "regarding yourself as *The* woman," "trying to embody a myth," "believing oneself to be" the real woman, maybe the only one, or imposing your gender norms to others. Lacan went as far as considering the too powerful identifications as madness. Believing too much in one's being is already to yield to complacency. If this holds for the paranoiac, who believes a little too much that he is who he is, feeling that nobody understands him, it is also true for the feminine subject who takes herself for "The" woman. The lack-of-being affects each subject and taking oneself for "The woman" is a kind of madness jeopardizing the bond to the other. But in truth, in practice, it turns out that, when a woman believes that "'The' woman exists," she does not place her in herself but in the Other. What matters then is the status of this Other. Because it seems as if, instead of consenting to this Other in herself, a woman placed her own foreignness in the Other. Such is the effect of splitting oneself in two, characteristic of femininity.

"I already know a thing or two. I know it's not clothes that make women beautiful or otherwise, nor beauty care, nor expensive creams, nor the distinction or costliness of their finery. I know the problem lies elsewhere. I don't know where it is. I only know it is not where women think."[2] This is the way Duras speaks of this other place where the question of a woman's desire is situated, which is not where she believes it is. She mentions this relation to the masquerade as displacing the issue rather than offering a truth on femininity. Coming from a writer and a woman who writes, Marguerite Duras' words say something that sheds light on the aphorism "'The' woman does not exist." When in 1970, Lacan says that "*The* woman doesn't exist," it resonates as a saying which leaves us puzzled and perplexed. This sentence shouldn't be read perhaps as a sententious axiom but rather as one would read a fragment from Heraclitus's writings. "It is not possible to step into the same river twice," "Everything gives way," "The woman doesn't exist." Perhaps it was Lacan's way of throwing a bottle in the ocean of discourses on "women" so as to crack this rigid idea of "The" woman as a paradigm.

"The woman does not exist" is not to be interpreted as one more truth or lie about "women," but as a way to make holes in the land of words and introduce another relation to existence than that which is based on universal principles. What Lacan emphasizes is this impossible access to the "The" of "The woman" and the necessity to follow a singular path, which leads each woman to become not "The" woman but "a" woman. He turns the experience of femininity into a phenomenon which cannot be universalized, which is "an objection to the universal,"[3] to use Jacques-Alain Miller's expression, and which never gives a woman access to an identity, but to a jouissance which breaks through every identity.

In what sense does the experience of feminine jouissance crack the relation to what one thought to be? As I am not-all [pas-toute] present in this place where others are, I can accept this part which does not recognize itself in any "We." Being not-all there, being also represented by an "elsewhere," a part of what I am does not enter discourse and yet it exists. Being overwhelmed, by such an experience at some point in one's life, is to feel that there is something of existence that eludes the universal principles that are imposed upon us, something which cannot express itself and which makes me feel as if I were split into two. Consenting to assume this part which is not represented in the group of beings who belong to the same species, or even in language, is to be able to do something else with it and not reject it or suffer from it as an exclusion from one's being. It means assuming the feminine part of one's existence as a joyful marginality.

To me, the aphorism "The woman does not exist" – suggestive of presocratic philosophy – is to be understood from this experience of splitting. It follows that a subject can, on the one hand, feel that he or she is connected to the others and to what is said in the world, and on the other hand, feels connected to something which has no meaning. *Vertigo*, by Alfred Hitchcock, is the film which stages such a splitting through Madeleine and Judy, a splitting between the blonde-haired girl and the red-haired girl, between the one who is dead and the one who is alive. But this splitting is dealt with from the point of view of a man, Scottie, fascinated by the one whose identity he can't grasp. After Hitchcock, David Lynch in *Mulholland Drive* (2001)[4] revisited the same theme, but from the point of view of a feminine subject. In my book *Les Amoureuses*, I dealt with the experience of desire as shown through the dream and the nightmare of a lost woman. I mention this unforgettable film only to add that the enigma of the message David Lynch aims at conveying is also knotted around the experience of splitting. This is what holds my attention in my investigation into the hidden spring of consent.

This mysterious film shows how a woman, here Diane Selwyn, rejects the splitting out of herself, by crediting another woman with a radiant femininity which, it seems to her, is beyond her reach. Diane's fate highlights this belief in the existence of "The" woman that lends weight to the Other woman, to the point, sometimes, where it causes such a fascination, that it leaves the subject mute about herself. In this film, the heroine is ensnared in her own fascination. The Other woman, who, in her eyes, possesses the secret of femininity, is the one in whom she rejects the excluded part of herself. The Other woman embodies the one who doesn't seem to have ever questioned herself about her femininity, a woman without anxiety, a woman, so to speak, by nature.

The relationship to the Other woman can go through different levels of intensity, from mere admiration – leading her to take an interest in the Other woman, in her appearance, her style, her relation to presence and absence, the way she has of being or not being, of revealing or concealing herself as she speaks – to deadly fascination. The subject then becomes petrified by what he or she does not make sense of. David Lynch's film is precisely about this fascination which becomes conspicuous in Diane's dream. Diane believes that "The" woman exists and that she is called Rita, already splitting into Rita/Camilla Rhodes within the dreamlike production of the dreamer. Diane splits into Betty/Rita in her own dream. She is both the dark-haired woman and the fair-haired one, the one who knows and the one who doesn't, the one who appears on the set and the one who hides so that no one can find her, the one who remembers and the one who suffers from amnesia about her identity.

Everything is then confused. Instead of consenting to this splitting within herself, Diane Selwyn rejects into the Other the foreignness she feels in herself. To her, Camilla's body has become the keeper of the mystery of desire.

The film is actually about a splitting between a part of oneself one can speak about and a part of oneself one cannot, even though we experience it, sometimes without even knowing where it leads us. This part about which one can say nothing, which confronts us to what we don't know about ourselves, we can try to get rid of it by rejecting it into the Other. But if we are to believe Lacan, what leads a subject to consent to the experience of femininity is, on the contrary, to be able to assume this dimension of otherness to oneself.

Experiencing femininity is not believing that the Other woman exists. This moment of belief is the sign that one meets with a difficulty in one's existence, a question about oneself. It is even perhaps the first step towards the experience of becoming different from what we are, other to oneself. Experiencing femininity has nothing to do either with making the others believe that "The" woman exists in oneself, even for make-believe, for playacting, for the theatre of the genders. It is in fact the reverse. To look like "The" woman, wanting to be the woman, pretending one knows much about feminine sexuality, desire, love, bears testimony to a relationship with the image and not with being. It can even be an ironical relation to femininity, so as not to feel concerned by this singular experience. It is a way to show that one doesn't believe in it, while limiting the question to the role and the masquerade.

A Jouissance "of her own"

Consenting to this part of ourselves, which is marked by opacity, and which can awaken like an ignored part of what we didn't know about ourselves when there is an encounter with desire or love, is not a matter of role-playing. In what sense does the experience of femininity have a link with consent which is necessary rather than contingent? In that the experience of femininity, as a subjective adventure, rests precisely on "consent." It does not rest on a biological program, nor is it reduced to a social assignment. It rests on a "*cum-sentire*," and this is why the aphorism "To yield is not to consent" has also a clinical and ethical import, beside its political dimension.

As I am nearing the end of my investigation of the frontier between "to yield" and "to consent," I am trying to grasp the stakes of consent from the feminine. But I must tear myself away from a kind of silence surrounding the question, to try and say something about it. I don't know if I will manage to shed light on it but at least, I will attempt to evoke it, drawing from what psychoanalysis, but also literature and the encounter with certain experiences have taught me. This experience of femininity is not just a "*cum-sentire*" as a sort of communion with the other, a *becoming one with the other*, a kind of perfect harmony. I believe that this experience is awaken by the body, the voice, the look of another, but mostly it is a "*cum-sentire*" which has to do with a certain "being-with" one's body, an experience of jouissance which is not necessarily sayable but nevertheless real.

So, what is this feminine jouissance which, in some respect, also severs my tongue, but on a different mode from that of trauma?

Some experience it in their sexual life, others in childbirth or motherhood, others still by devoting themselves to a cause which makes them feel a kind of ecstasy, others through a form of writing or creation. This experience, which is both real and unsayable, sometimes occurs without the subject always recognizing what is happening to them. As if something was happening that severed the subject's tongue, so intense is the event of jouissance. Besides, it is not because a woman talks a lot that she manages to speak about it, about this experience she is going through and which at the same time she silences without being aware of it. This is why, those who do manage to say something about it, through a narrative, a work of art, or an invention, enlighten us with their valuable contributions about what can only be hinted at or "half-said," to borrow Lacan's neologism. That's why, here too, it is at times necessary to go through silence.

Those who manage to transmit something about it, don't enlighten us from the position of the Other woman who wants us to believe that she knows. They don't enlighten us by cloaking themselves in knowledge. They enlighten us by telling us about what they don't know. They show us the way by not silencing what they can't say. These women are brave and daring enough to bring into existence this zone of femininity as an experience that breaks with social rules. They don't speak of what they know but of what confronts them to an absence of knowledge. They say what they went through, and this has more to do with a testimony than with a theory or with knowledge. As far as I am concerned, this is what moves me.

What Lacan calls "femininity" is not an attribute, something one has or not, possessions, riches, opportunities, something one would own and others wouldn't. What he calls "femininity" or, more precisely "a jouissance of her own,"[5] has to do with an encounter at the level of the body itself, caused by the other. A form of jouissance that makes one feel a sort of plus, "more life" in one's body, and produces a splitting in one's being. Feeling that one is both "here" and "not here," present and absent, other to oneself. The place from which I feel absent to myself is not, however, a place where I disappear, as in trauma, but a place where I experience what is happening in my existence as outside the symbolic world, excluded by the nature of words, but present all the same in another place. As if beyond the world of language, which is something like dry land, there was an ocean of jouissance. The littoral, this place which takes us to the seashore, is also a way to approach this jouissance without drowning in it.

There is no "being woman," a state one would reach, following a rite of passage and once and for all, or some kind of bliss; there are only singular moments, scraps of experiences of this jouissance, moments of encounters, of words, emotions, which make you feel this thing beyond desire and which carry desire away with them. What Lacan calls *femininity* has nothing to do with an identity but rather with an event, an adventure, a back-and-forth movement, a flutter between presence and absence, which confronts the subject with a gentle vertigo. It is a form of splitting where I can feel that I have a part within me that is inscribed within the other's world, where I am on dry land, while at the same time, another part evades what I can tell the other about myself, a part which lets itself be carried away by the movement of the waters.

What is to be done with this part that makes me other to myself, a part which means a lot to me, and which I experience as being excluded from the whole, and which can exclude me from it too? What is to be done with this impossibility to recognize myself wholly in some established knowledge, in a theory, in a discourse? Reject it? Deny it? Forget it? Or take the risk to live it, explore it and experience it? It is from this phenomenon of exclusion of this jouissance supplementary to the world of words, that I am trying to grasp something of Lacan's way to shed light on consent from the feminine. It is a form of jouissance which is not caused by a particular organ but affects the whole being or rather, the living body as a speaking body, and which always remains ignored by the "we."

It is in this zone of one's existence that the "letting it happen" goes along with both a jouissance and trust in the other. It is the same "letting it happen" that I have already mentioned with Annie Ernaux's simple passion. It is a "letting it happen" that threads its way one day, for a first time, and leaves a mark.

Consent, a Displacement

"It's dark in the studio, but she doesn't ask him to open the shutters. She doesn't feel anything in particular, no hate, no repugnance either, so probably it's already desire. But she doesn't know it. She agreed to come as soon as he asked her the previous evening."[6]

When I read *The Lover* for the first time, I wasn't fifteen yet. The novel was so popular that it was regarded as a romantic story for young girls prone to daydreaming, compared to the poetic complexity of *The Ravishing of Lol Stein*, for example, but now, with the benefit of hindsight, my opinion about it is altogether different. In this novel, Marguerite Duras managed to explore an area of the experience of feminine jouissance which is not confined to the love utopia depicted in fairytales. *The Ravishing of Lol Stein* is the account of a trauma, of the abduction of a being, of a body collapsing the day when, before her eyes, her love partner leaves with another woman; it is the account of a "suffering without subject,"[7] a woman, no longer in her body, who becomes silent. *The Lover*, by contrast, is the account of a young woman's consent to feminine jouissance, a young woman who discovers sexuality in the arms of a man who worships her.

It is hardly a love story. Rather a story about the awakening of desire. The man from Cholon, who owns a black limousine, professes his love for her, but she isn't in the same region of love. She doesn't say that she loves him because she doesn't know if she can really love someone. She knows that she has followed him, that she has consented to follow him to let go of herself in his arms.

Marguerite Duras manages to write about this splitting of being by introducing a double time dimension: she is an experienced, mature woman, who writes in the first-person and revisits the encounter with sexuality of a fifteen-year-old who appears in the third person. But she also writes about this splitting, by bringing to life the "I" of the fifteen- and a half-year-old young girl and by introducing the "she," to speak about this stranger she was to herself at that age.

A jouissance "of her own."

Between this "she" and this "I," Duras explores the gap, which is also the gap of feminine jouissance, which means that a woman experiences a jouissance which is not hers, but rather "of her own." The "I" therefore becomes, by way of the experience of jouissance, a "she," other to herself. What is strange about this narrative is that it is hardly a love story. It is first and foremost an encounter with of desire. The young woman can't say that she really loves her Chinese lover, whom she meets every afternoon in Saigon. "She's where she has to be, placed here. She feels a tinge of fear. It's as if this must be not only what she expects, but also what had to happen especially to her."[8]

Her consent placed her in a different location, this room where they met in the mugginess of the afternoon, a room where, from then on and forever, she could escape the people she thought she belonged to so far: her mother and her two brothers. "As soon as she got into the black car she knew: she's excluded from the family for the first time and forever. From now on they will no longer know what becomes of her."[9] As she becomes other to herself, "a" woman in the arms of a man madly in love with her body, she separates herself from this "whole" she formed with her family, the whole being the mother with her children. "She pays close attention to externals, to the light, to the noise of the city in which the room is immersed. He's trembling. At first he looks at her as though he expects her to speak, but she doesn't. So he doesn't do anything either, doesn't undress her, says he loves her madly, says it very softly."[10]

A first time. Between silence, whisper and consent.
Destitution.
"Yes."

Notes

 1 Virginia Woolf, *A Woman's College from the Outside*, Bookclassic, 1926, p. 6.
 2 Marguerite Duras, *The Lover*, Transl. Barbara Bray, London, Penguin, p. 22.
 3 Jacques-Alain Miller, "L'Un tout seul" [The One All-Alone], *L'Orientation lacanienne*, Teaching pronounced at the Department of Psychoanalysis of the University of Paris 8, Course of 25 May 2011. Unpublished.
 4 See Clotilde Leguil, *Les Amoureuses, voyage au bout de la féminité*, Paris, Seuil, 2009.
 5 Jacques Lacan, *The Seminar of Jacques Lacan. Book XX, Encore*, Ed. J.-A. Miller, Transl. Bruce Fink, W.W. Norton & Co., New York/London, 1999, p. 74. Translation modified.
 6 Marguerite Duras, *The Lover*, Transl. Barbara Bray, Penguin, London, 1986, p. 40.
 7 Marguerite Duras, *The Ravishing of Lol Stein*, Transl. Richard Seaver, Pantheon, New York, 1986, p. 22.
 8 Duras, p. 40.
 9 Duras, p. 39.
10 Duras, p. 40.

Chapter 12

Mad Concessions

Experiencing this desire, which is a desire of the other as well as a desire to be desired, is not to submit to the other or to alienate oneself; it is to take the risk of consenting to this turmoil which makes me foreign to myself. There lies the ambiguity, the proximity, and, at the same time, the boundary between "yielding" and "consenting." In Lacan's perspective, the experience of femininity has to do with an encounter with a jouissance that permeates the body, and to which one consents. The experience of "yielding," of trauma, has to do with a jouissance imposed by the other and which also somehow causes an earthquake in the subject's body, but one to which the subject does not consent. This is the difference.

This is where my journey leads me. Yes, there is a dangerous proximity between "yielding" and "consenting" because in these two kinds of experiences, expressed by the infinitive form of the verbs, there is an encounter with jouissance and with a form of "letting it happen." From now on, the enigma bears on the question: "why does one let it happen?" even when the body says "no"? This is the knot.

In consent, jouissance is the event brought about in an unexpected way by a "yes." In the subjective cession, the jouissance extracted from the body is the traumatic event produced while the body itself says "no."

Examining the war trauma may have helped us grasp how wide the gap between these two body events can be. I can say that I have somehow prepared myself to the consented jouissance. I may be anxious after saying "yes," because I feel I let go of myself to try something new. But this is a "yes" which opens up a path towards an experience of life. In contrast, however, I am never prepared to the jouissance which is not consented, the other's jouissance which is also imposed on my body. When it happens, I am estranged from myself, in shame, in silence, in fright. The encounter with otherness in me is inverted in an encounter with a forcing by the other.

Letting Go of Oneself and Falling Under the Sway of the Other

As I pointed out at the beginning of this essay, the gracefulness of Vanessa Springora's book *Consent*, lies in placing itself at the level of what it means, for a very young girl who dreams of becoming a woman, to encounter the Other's desire.

DOI: 10.4324/9781003536956-12

As one reads *Consent*, one grasps what it means to consent to something which goes beyond what one thought one had consented to. One grasps that consenting to the Other's desire does not go without anxiety. Consenting to femininity is always a crossing over for a young woman. The first encounter, during which a young girl loses her virginity, leaves indelible marks on her body. Vanessa Springora's story might have been reminiscent of Duras. The young girl had consented to have a first lover, older than herself, expecting him to carry her away elsewhere, far from her mother, towards the woman she felt like becoming. But the analogy stops here. If for a time, she thought herself loved, although disoriented by the turn this love is taking in terms of sexual relationships, she afterwards opens her eyes and realizes that she has never been the object of his love, that everything was engineered, planned so that she should become the object of his jouissance.

V. writes that by virtue of the desire she felt, she never identified with a victim. She believed that the Other's desire wished her own desire to awaken, but she was deceived. And since becoming a woman requires this consent to be desired, sexual abuse is a betrayal of consent itself. The traumatic effect doesn't only stem from being prematurely initiated into sexual practices which were not for someone her age, besides by a fifty-year old man while she was fourteen. What caused the trauma is the fact that she desired this man and thought she was loved by him. It is on this point of vulnerability that the poison of the bad encounter has an effect. Because what she consents to then, by virtue of the desire she feels and the love in which she believes, is forcing. This is deceit. She thought she was an object of desire and love. In actual fact, she became a pure object of jouissance for the other.

The crossing of the boundary between "consenting" and "yielding" is located where letting go of oneself leaves a space in which one may eventually fall under the sway of the other.[1] Because falling under the sway of the other requires one to let go of oneself first. This first-person narrative recounts a situation where consent paved the way for trauma.

The bad encounter came as an answer to an existential wavering in a secondary-school pupil caught between a mother she doted on, who was slightly lost and disoriented, with whom she was at one, and a father who remained indifferent to her existence. It is at the very moment when she is waiting for a man, as one would wait for a father, that this man appears, turning her into his prey. The father she encounters is neither a loving father nor a desiring one, he is the father of jouissance: the one who exploits the fascination he exerts on her as a writer, satisfying thereby his own sexual urges. After the bad encounter, she suffered anxiety attacks, an anorexic episode, and a moment of depersonalization, a testimony to the emotional earthquake that this first story which was not a love story for her.

"How long had it been since I lost all trace of myself?"[2] Losing trace of oneself is a truly feminine experience, which can condemn a woman to nonexistence. Because the bad encounter has reenacted the trauma retroactively, the trauma when, as a child, at night, she heard a violent scene between her mother and her lover. The words "turn over" addressed by a lover to her mother will come back to her, uttered by this man whom, at fourteen, she will not be able to escape, just as one can't escape an imperative of ferocious jouissance.

This book written by a woman who finally got through thanks to a headmistress who gave a significant place to her subjective tragedy, and thanks to a man she could trust, shows us that the question of desire and jouissance may lead to a place where the boundary between "consenting" and "yielding" is blurred. It is at this point that the distinction becomes urgent.

There is undeniably a dangerous proximity between the two experiences and Vanessa Springora's intimate account shows precisely how intertwined consent and cession are. As if, sometimes, in the life of a subject, consent, with its dizzying, opaque, and enigmatic aspects, could be the shortest route to cession. It does not mean that "consenting" becomes "yielding" and "yielding" "consenting." It means that a pact has been betrayed.

Thinking Oneself Loved, Going Astray

Vanessa Springora asserts that at fourteen she was "consenting." She was in love and "felt adored."[3] This is where the notion of consent demonstrates its value and its function, in its relationship to feminine jouissance. For the feminine subject, love is a condition of jouissance. In the name of this love, consent leads to the biggest concessions. Thinking oneself loved is to feel a new relation to one's body based on the other's love. There lies the enigma: for a woman, "consent to become a sexual object" is entangled with "the experience of thinking oneself loved." This is what *Consent* by Vanessa Springora shows. Her consent, her letting go of herself because she thinks herself loved while she in fact is the plaything of the other's pervert strategy, becomes instrumentalized by a man who has become a master in the relationships with young girls under 15. There, letting go of oneself gives way to falling under the sway of the other.

When a woman "thinks herself loved" to the point of forgetting herself, she complies with a demand from the superego and wishes to "do everything" to be loved totally. Consent to desire gives way to a limitlessness in love. Madness results from an absence of limits to the concessions a woman or a young girl, can make[4] in the name of a "thinking herself loved" by a man: leaving the people she loved, consenting to become the object of a sexuality in which she finds no satisfaction, going as far as considering to travel with him to Manila, though she knows he practices sexual tourism, fully aware that he has written about pedophilia and yet turning a blind eye to it, not daring to "submit a desire,"[5] which would break the routine of the mechanical nature of the lovemaking he imposed upon her.

One day, an awakening of sorts occurs: "I awake to a new reality." Rebellion follows as well as her flat dismissal of the man who regards her as mad and hysterical. Then, at fifteen and a half, alone, out of his grip, she describes the episode of depersonalization she experiences: "A dreadful sensation like being ripped from the realm of the living, but in slow motion."[6] What she yielded to has nothing to do with what she consented to. "Consenting" may lead to "Yielding" without one even realizing that the boundary has been crossed.

At the heart of the boundary between "yielding" and "consenting," there is the sexual and psychological trauma. If psychoanalysis has sometimes served to muddy the waters, it is due to the fact that, in the context of a claim to jouissance which ignores the drive and its effects on the other, Freud's discovery and Lacan's developments were not properly understood. The problem of sexual trauma such as is tackled by psychoanalysis, and this since the birth of psychoanalysis with Freud, is not only that of consent, of ambiguity, of the "yes," and the "no," but it is also the problem of "yielding." I showed this with the case of Emma. It is not because Freud extended the scope of sexuality, speaking of infantile sexuality, that he underestimated the importance of sexual trauma, and even less thought that a child's sexual life bore any relation whatsoever to that of an adult's.[7] Confronting a traumatic situation has nothing to do with an identifiable behavior, but with a subjective cession, a disappearance whose impact can only be grasped afterwards, when time has allowed the subject to come back from where he had disappeared.

How Psychoanalysis can be Misused in the Service of the Drive

The boundary between "yielding and "consenting" may have disappeared because in the 1970s and 1980s, psychoanalysis was used by some who conflated desire and the drive. Subsequently, at the heart of the sexual liberation, the confusion remained in the name of a so- called ethics of desire which claimed its adherence to Lacan's theory, conflating unfettered jouissance and desire. One of Lacan's major contributions to the question of sexual trauma is to have radically distinguished between "desire" and "the drive." In this respect, I can remember a remark by Jacques-Alain Miller in 2011, during the Strauss-Kahn sex-assault case, when comments came thick and fast about seduction, gallantry, housemaids being tupped, and the alleged consent of the hotel maid of the Sofitel in New York. "Being a man of desire and being a man of the drive are not the same thing. The drive is the drive of the One and it is not at all in tune with the other's desire; one could even argue that at this level, the inexistence of this other is conspicuous."[8] True, for a woman, encountering a man of desire is not the same thing as encountering a man of the drive. It is not because the drive and desire are tied that desire must be reduced to the drive and confused with it. Desire for psychoanalysis is not Sadean desire. The drive leads you to no longer take the other's consent into consideration or to instrumentalize this consent as one can do with minors. It has nothing to do with desire, which is always a desire of the other, namely, caught in the relation to the Other.

In 1960, Lacan wrote: "Only love allows jouissance to condescend to desire."[9] Without love, it is indeed not necessary for jouissance to condescend to desire; everything is going well from the point of view of the drive, by short-circuiting all that is connected to desire, and by seeking to draw enjoyment from the other's body, whatever their consent. The drive is without the other and there, it is true "everything is allowed." In that respect, it can also devastate whoever finds themselves in the position of a pure object of jouissance. It is never in the name of desire that everything is allowed, but always in the name of the drive, which sometimes can appear under the guise of freedom. When the drive is not tied with the relation to the other, it becomes destructive, a death drive, as Freud put it. The drive of one destroys the subjectivity of another by violating it.

In the experience of an analysis, desire emerges when one tears oneself away from the death drive inherent in the symptom. A desire breaks away, extracts itself from it, in accordance with the subject's choice. The experience of an analysis results in extracting desire so that it should not be crushed by the drive. Psychoanalysis is related to an ascesis of desire.[10] It has to do with "the subjective production of a void,"[11] which leaves room for the lack and has nothing to do with an encouragement to enjoy without limits. In brief, psychoanalysis doesn't encourage you to enjoy without restriction, it encourages you to *trust* your desire to *mistrust* your drive.

Such misuse of psychoanalysis which may even be called an instrumentalization of psychoanalysis in the service of perversion, could also be seen in 1977, when a number of prominent intellectuals took a stand in favour of the decriminalization of relationships between adults and children. The fact is mentioned by Vanessa Springora. In 1977, the petition "About a trial" was signed by Barthes, Deleuze, Beauvoir, Sartre, Glücksmann, Aragon.... The petition was clearly about a forcing of consent, in other words it advocated a presumption of consent for children, to the advantage of the adults' sexual desire. Consent was used in the service of the drive. The same year, as Vanessa Springora points out, "A call for the Revision of the Penal Code Regarding Relationships Between Minors and Adults,"[12] was signed by eighty people, with Françoise Dolto, Louis Althusser, and Jacques Derrida adding their support to those who had signed the earlier petition. To assert the difference in nature between "yielding" and "consenting" is also to show the error of those who considered that sexual relationships initiated by adults towards children or teenagers meant consent, in the name of the Sovereign Good that desire (mistaken for jouissance) was supposed to be.

In that respect, it is surprising that, ten years earlier, in the middle of the May 1968 events in France, no intellectual should have considered drawing up a petition to support Gabrielle Russier, a French teacher in Marseilles who had been in a love relationship with one of her pupils who was a minor, and as a result, was incarcerated and eventually dismissed from her post. In the end, she took her own life.[13] As if, because it was a case of a woman in love – a woman carried away by her passion and slightly lost – and not a question of controlled sexuality or a minor's sexual education, then indifference prevails over revolt. Free enjoyment of all the bodies is obviously a utopia which is close to the Sadean morals, about which Lacan recalls in his seminar on the *Ethics of Psychoanalysis*, that Sade advocated a right to jouissance "without" the other's consent. Vanessa Springora uses the terms "adrift" and "blindness" to describe the signatories who, she recalls, would later apologize. I would also use the term "adrift" in the sense that jouissance sends us adrift: it leads us where satisfaction is encountered in a repetitive way. For Lacan, the ethics of psychoanalysis is precisely what brings us where we won't be led astray by the demand of the drive. Ascesis of desire.

As I was reading Vanessa Springora's book, I grasped at last, in what sense "thinking herself loved" may lead a woman to an absence of limits to the concessions she can make for *a* man, "of her body, her soul, her possessions."[14] This is where the shift is. Between "consenting" and "yielding" lies the range of the concessions, those I can make because I think I am loved and, at the same time, those I make because of the anxiety I experience, the feeling that, if I don't give everything, I may no longer be loved. Conceding is then renouncing one's desire to make of the Other's supposed jouissance the hypothetical sign of love, which is in fact already lost.

This love, which leads to a crossing of the boundary between consenting and yielding, is not in the active voice but in the passive voice. There lies the ambiguity, between the passive voice of the jouissance inherent in "thinking oneself loved" and the concessions a woman can make in the name of that belief.

Notes

1 "*où la déprise de soi laisse une place à l'emprise de l'autre.*"
2 Vanessa Springora, *Consent: A Memoir*, Transl. Natasha Lehrer, Harper Collins, 2021, p. 157.
3 Springora, p. 45.
4 Jacques Lacan, *Television: A Challenge to the Psychoanalytic Establishment*, Ed. J. Copjec, Transl. Denis Hollier, Rosalind Krauss, and Annette Michelson, W.W. Norton & Co., New York, 1990, p. 40.
5 Springora, p. 111.
6 Springora, p. 156.
7 Serge Tisseron, "le désir peut exister, mais cela ne change rien à ce qui est permis et défendu", *Le Monde*, 22 January 2020. "Desire may exist, but it doesn't change anything as to what is allowed and what is forbidden."
8 Jacques-Alain Miller, "L'Un tout seul [The One-All Alone], L'orientation lacanienne, Teaching pronounced at the Department of Psychoanalysis at the University of Paris 8, Course of 25 May 2011. Unpublished.
9 Jacques Lacan, *The Seminar of Jacques Lacan. Book X, Anxiety*, Ed. J.-A. Miller, Transl. A. R. Price, Cambridge, Polity, 2014, p. 179.
10 See the end of *The Seminar of Jacques Lacan. Book VII, The Ethics of Psychoanalysis*, lesson XXIV, Ed. J.-A. Miller, Transl. Dennis Porter, W.W. Norton & Co, New York/ London, 1992.
11 Jacques Lacan, *The Seminar of Jacques Lacan. Book XII, The Object of Psychoanalysis*, lesson of 15 December 1965. Unpublished.
12 Springora, p. 50.
13 See "L'affaire Gabrielle Russier, un amour hors la loi", *Le Monde*, summer series by Pascale Robert-Diard and Joseph Beauregard, July-August 2020.
14 Lacan, p. 40.

Chapter 13

Beyond Rebellion, Consenting to Say

As we approach the end of this exploration, I can see that, above and beyond the "no" of rebellion, the springs of consent have something to do with anxiety [*angoisse*]. When it comes to consent, it is the field of desire and jouissance that is at stake.

It seems to me that the Freudian term "superego" helps grasp this strange logic inherent in consent, which can lead one to cross a boundary with a point of no-return. It is not only the Other who puts pressure on me, it's also the Other in me, which Freud named the *superego*. This silent inner voice subjects me to a demand that I don't choose. The superego is this authoritarian voice which silences me and wants me to become an accomplice to the drive, the drive in the Other as well as mine. The superego prevents me from rebelling by imposing silence when my desire is ill-treated, held in contempt, and sometimes abused. But the crossing of the boundary between what I desire and what I impose upon myself is shown somewhere in my body. I experience fear and anxiety at the idea of losing what I believed I would gain by consenting. But the question is: what am I afraid of losing by refusing to consent to what I do not desire?

Consenting "in the name of"

The question I will ask now at the end of this essay which made me delve into the depth of consent, is the following: in the name of what does one let it happen? As I have shown, the crux of the problem lies in the act of 'letting it happen," an experience which ranges from consent to "let it happen" to being forced and under the sway of someone. That a child should submit himself or herself to an adult who assaults them, does not result from sexual consent, but always from trust in the Other and sometimes from a feeling of fright at the idea that they could escape something which is already perceived as an effraction. Were it the result of consent, it would be consenting to love and to the bond with the other, as a founding principle of existence. It is precisely this first consent which is betrayed by the abuser.

As I am writing the final chapter of this book, the publication of *La Familia Grande*[1] by Camille Kouchner takes me back to the roots of the enigmatic experience of consent, where submitting to the other occurs. Each written testimony

DOI: 10.4324/9781003536956-13

opens new possibilities to give voice to one's experience. Here, Camille Kouchner, feeling "a vast sense of guilt for being alive,"[2] revisits, thirty years after it happened, a situation where she "submitted to another." At that time, she had no choice to do otherwise. She was the one who was compelled by her stepfather to act as his accomplice as he committed sexual abuse on her twin brother. "I was fourteen and I let it happen. I was fourteen and, by letting it happen, I might as well have done it myself. I was fourteen and I knew and I didn't say nothing."[3]

The abuse can begin very simply, in a surreptitious way, from what is heard or known and insinuates itself into the heart of a person's private life, here a fourteen-year-old teenager. "He came into my bedroom, and thanks to his tenderness and the close bond between us, thanks to the trust I had in him, he very gently, using no violence, instiled silence in me."[4] Being under someone's sway, the subject is silenced without even being aware of it. This is the abuse. But trusting someone when one is fourteen is a condition without which it is impossible to find a place to be. To have faith in the words of someone one trusts, is also to believe in the world. How is it possible to live otherwise? The specificity of the pervert not only consists in deriving enjoyment from somebody else's body without their consent, but also in violating their psyche, by making them believe that deep down, they consent to what destroys them and to the disgrace imposed upon them. Here, while Camille Kouchner's brother becomes a victim of incest, she also becomes the victim of another abuse which is committed without violence, sealing her lips. "My guilt was the guilt of consent. I was guilty of not having stopped my stepfather, of not having understood that incest was forbidden."[5]

Must we think that the teenager who keeps silent – as her brother asks her to, by saying to her: "if you speak, I will die" – consents? Does complying with the other's requests mean that she consents? The circumstances in which incest occurred have already condemned the teenager to a crippling fear. Her grandmother has just committed suicide. The foundations of the teenager's world are becoming unstable. Her mother sinks into depression and can no longer parent her. It is right at this moment of family distress that Camille's adored stepfather chooses to act.

Thus, the fourteen-year-old girl fell silent, utterly dazed, under the sway of this man who had come to replace the father she missed. She fell silent, fearful that another tragic event might follow, that suicide might recur in the family, that of her mother, critically weakened by the loss of her own mother. This book teaches us that a subject does not always have the means to say "no." The guilt of having been unable to say "no," the guilt of having said "yes" to what she has not understood, by keeping silent, is from now on, what haunts her, the hydra, as she calls it, which poisons her. She did not know that incest was forbidden. But wasn't it the role of her stepfather who acted as father, to embody this interdiction?

This in-depth study of the roots of consent shows us that at the origin of guilt and of psychical and sexual trauma, there is an experience of "letting it happen" which comes back to the subject as an enigma. In the name of what did she let it happen? She let it happen in the name of what her stepfather had himself christened the *familia grande*. There is always a "in the name of" which leads one to consent and condone. There's always a "in the name of" which prompts one to let it happen. There is always a "in the name of" which encourages us to abdicate as subjects, in order to defend the indivisibility of the family, the undivided condition of an imaginary love, the undivided condition of a community.

Disobeying

Nevertheless, it is also "in the name of," that the subject can one day wake up and, at last, disobey the submission which he or she imposed upon themselves. If it is "in the name of" the *familia grande* and the love for her mother – a love which could be described as an *impossible love*,[6] to use Christine Angot's words – that Camille Kouchner consented to keep silent, it may also be "in the name" of what it means for her to be a sister and a mother, and also because she feared that silence should be passed on to the next generation, that she managed to disobey.

In the way of Antigone, who will never yield and goes all the way to fulfil her responsibilities, from her own position, Camille Kouchner writes about what lay behind the *familia grande*, thirty years after the event happened. This book represents an act of courage and raises the question of disobedience at a time – the 1970s – when freedom reigned supreme and when the motto "banning is banned" dominated the *Zeitgeist* of the times. This personal account is also strengthened by the fact that it sheds light on what lurks behind the claim for freedom at all costs: an unleashing of jouissance, which eventually silences the subject who desires something else.

Fear is what is felt when it comes to tearing the veil covering up what seemed to represent the world. Fear explains why the subject sometimes prefer to turn a blind eye on what makes the world vile, as Lacan said. The price to pay to access one's own "I" is therefore another form of consent: a consent to take the risk of losing a world one has believed in. At last, thirty years later, Camille Kouchner manages to break free from this silence, and to "poison the hydra by finishing this book."[7]

The instrumentalization of consent in totalitarian regimes is, in the political field, akin to the instrumentalization of consent in sexual life. Because it is after all a pact of trust, both in the intimate consent and in the political consent and this pact involves the relation to speech. This dangerous closeness between yielding and consenting is also about a blurring of boundaries in myself, between what I can accept, what I can give, what I can even sacrifice for the other and which will destroy me.

How far can consent take me? Should I go so far as renouncing my own desire? This may be the sign that something is taking place to which I can, from now on, say "no." As Albert Camus wrote: to rebel is to say "no" and at the same time to assert something. Rebellion is thus likened to an awakening. Saying "no" implies crossing a line which is already, at the same time, a "yes."

Rebelling, when consent has led to trauma, is to find oneself again.

It's to affirm: "I am here again," I have not disappeared. It means tearing oneself away from the hold someone has on you, from the shame, from the fear of losing oneself a second time by speaking up. It sometimes implies being ready to confront the loss of a world, the world of the family or of love, in the name of a greater principle, which is the possibility to say "I."

Rebellion may take the shape of a collective "no," to express and lodge somewhere what has happened. However, it is more powerful when someone finds his or her own singular voice. It opens onto what can only be expressed in the first person to a particular Other. Because, ultimately, what happened, happened to me. By writing about it, by speaking about it to another who will be able to hear it, by attempting to say it, I also give greater value to the traumatic trace and to what left a mark on my body, not allowing anyone else to speak on my behalf. I give it such a value that I would not reveal it to just anyone or in just any circumstance. Writing can be a "room of one's own" that enables me to reconnect with the world of the Other, without silencing that which broke into my own world.

I am here. Again. I can speak. In a place which, for me, has become the place where my own words have emerged.

Albert Camus considered rebellion as a genuine movement whose significance was all the greater as the movement remained faithful to its initial momentum. Behind the "no," there is also a "yes," an assertion of one's being. This is perhaps where the "We" must give way to the "I" who manages to face up to the intimate history, confronting what can be said and what is unsayable. This is where language, with all its power and flaws, succeeds in giving a place to the trauma.

As I was in the process of writing this book, plunging into the depths of consent, I discovered that there was a legal vacuum about the term consent. In French Law, whatever the age of the individual, there is no such thing as the presumption of non-consent. Acknowledging non-consent based on a specific age would be a violation of the presumption of innocence. Consequently, non-consent must be proven. And the only proof accepted by the law today is the use of force.[8]

The paradox is that by attempting to prove the absence of consent of a child or a teenager who has yielded to someone's sway, one reinforces their trauma. Once again, their consent is being instrumentalized by assuming that it caused trauma.

The point I have reached shows that restricting yourself to looking for a proof of non-consent in order to assert the reality of a sexual abuse, is failing to see the distinction between yielding and consenting. Abuse is always a betrayal of consent. The more intimate question which is outside the purview of the law is: "in the name of what" could the subject let it happen?

The feeling of guilt experienced by the subject is the point where submitting to the other was possible because of a belief in being loved, a belief in the undivided condition of the family which led the subject to force themselves as a strange response to the Other's forcing.

What happened there can't exclusively be redressed within the scope of the justice system, although on this point French lawmaking bears witness to the misrecognition of the psychological causes and consequences of abuse. Being granted victim status is not enough to recover from a trauma. As for being denied this status, it is tantamount to facing trauma a second time, because what is then termed a damage has not been acknowledged. Daring to say something from a place where my consent has given way to a cession, is also taking a risk, the risk of compounding the trauma. Camille Kouchner shows that she took this risk, the risk of speaking, of revealing a truth, and, several years before writing this book, the risk of seeing her loved ones, those who would rather continue to turn a blind eye on the events, backfiring on her.

Therefore, it is necessary sometimes to give back to speech a value it thought it no longer had. This is what psychoanalysis does. Breaking away from the "in the name of what" one condemned oneself to silence is to go through the confusion of discourses and find again a speech that reknits the thread of the real. That's why the person I will choose to address and the words which for the first time will resonate for me, will become new moorings for my being.

Consenting to say is to overcome fright.

Consenting to say is to be able to confront the past and not run away before anxiety.

Consenting to speak is to read those mysterious traces that remain forever waiting to be spelt. Like letters which have lost their original place, being no longer a part of any text, any sentence, any alphabet, letters marking the body and its way of being alive, letters which are the stigmata of the irreversible.

Consenting again is to say "yes" again.

Notes

1 Camille Kouchner, *The Familia Grande: A Memoir*, Transl. Adriana Hunter, Other Press, 2022.
2 Kouchner, p. 63.
3 Kouchner, p. 92.
4 Kouchner, p. 54.
5 Kouchner, p. 64.
6 Christine Angot, *An Impossible Love*, Archipelago Books, New York, 2021.
7 Angot, p. 99.
8 See *Appendix*.

Appendix[1]

Following the legal and ethical debates on the issue of consent for minors, after the publication of Camille Kouchner's book *The Familia Grande* (2021),[2] but also before that, Vanessa Springora's book *Consent* (2020), and one month after the French publication of this essay *Céder n'est pas consentir* (March 2021), on Thursday, 15 April 2021, the French Parliament eventually introduced an age threshold for non-consent at fifteen years old.

It is worth remembering that, prior to 2021, the French law defined rape by constraint and not by absence of consent. It was up to the victims to prove their non-consent even if they were minors.

The presumption of non-consent for minors under fifteen is therefore an essential legal advancement regarding sexual violence.

This law reinforces the protection of minors from sexual violence, establishing an age threshold for non-consent at fifteen and eighteen in case of incest. The Senate's proposed text was unanimously approved by the National Assembly (94 votes for, none against). Minister for Justice Eric Dupont-Moretti declared that the change was a historic breakthrough, three years after the Schiappa bill. In 2018, Marlène Schiappa, then France's Secretary of State for Gender Equality, had proposed, within the bill against sexist and sexual acts of violence, to establish an age of sexual non-consent. However, the measure was abandoned when the Constitutional Council failed to ratify it.

The new 2021 law redefined rape of underage children. It is no longer based on the three classical criteria in law (namely, threat, constraint, and surprise) but on the *a priori* non-consent of minors under fifteen. The sexual consent of a child with an adult no longer needs to be examined. Magistrates no longer need to ask the trick question of whether or not a child has consented. They will not need to prove that the adult made use of violence, threat, constraint, or surprise, as previously demanded by the criminal code. They will have to prove that the adult knew the child was under fifteen.

The law, which was enacted in April 2021, introduces an age threshold of fifteen under which any act of penetration by an adult will be considered a rape, a crime with a twenty-year prison sentence. A clause nicknamed "Romeo et Juliette" was added so that freely consented adolescent love-affairs should not be penalised.

Sanctions only apply if there is a difference of age of at least five years between the minor (who is under fifteen) and the adult.

French writer Christine Angot initiated a debate on the issue of the age of minority (eighteen years old) regarding incest. She advocates the prohibition of incest regardless of the age of the individual. This is also the position of this essay.[3]

Notes

1 This appendix was added for the publication of the Spanish translation of *Céder n'est pas consentir* following the change in legislation regarding the non-consent of minors, in April 2021, one month after the French publication of this essay (cf. the two articles in the French daily newspaper *Le Monde*: https://www.lemonde.fr/societe/article/2021/04/15/violences-sexuelles-le-parlement-adopte-une-loi-fixant-le-seuil-de-non-consentement-a-15-ans_6076933_3224.html et https://www.lemonde.fr/idees/article/2021/03/05/inceste-pedocriminalite-de-l-enfant-coupable-a-l-enfant-victime-la-lente-reconnaissance-du-non-consentement_6072031_3232.html [Retrieved November 2024.]

2 Cf. https://www.radiofrance.fr/franceinter/podcasts/l-heure-bleue/le-consentement-avec-camille-kouchner-et-clotilde-leguil-1780421 [Retrieved November 2024.]

3 Cf. https://www.liberation.fr/idees-et-debats/clotilde-leguil-dans-le-consentement-amoureux-et-sexuel-il-y-a-toujours-une-part-de-risque-et-dinconnu-20210409_MGQORJNSH-VHWRJG4IVUD6HTPNE/ [Retrieved November 2024.]

Bibliography

Christine Angot, *An Impossible Love*, Archipelago Books, New York, 2021.

Aharon Appelfeld, *The Story of a Life*, Transl. Aloma Halter, Penguin Books, London, 2004.

Albert Camus, *The Rebel: An Essay on Man in Revolt*, Transl. Anthony Bower, Vintage, 1992.

Confucius, *The Analects of Confucius*, R. Eno, 2015.

Gilles Deleuze, *Présentation de Sacher-Masoch*, Minuit, Paris, 1967, p. 18. *Masochism: Coldness and Cruelty*, 1989.

Marguerite Duras, *The Lover*, Transl. Barbara Bray, London, Penguin.

Marguerite Duras, *The Ravishing of Lol Stein*, Transl. Richard Seaver, Pantheon, New York, 1986.

Annie Ernaux, *Simple Passion*, Transl. Tania Leslie, Fitzcarraldo Editions, 2021.

Geneviève Fraisse, *Du consentement*, Seuil, Paris, 2017.

Sigmund Freud, "Beyond the Pleasure Principle" (1920) in *The Standard Edition of the Complete Psychological Works of Sigmund Freud*, Transl. James Strachey, Vol. XVIII, Vintage Classics, London, 2001.

Sigmund Freud, "Civilization and Its Discontents", in *The Standard Edition of the Complete Psychological Works of Sigmund Freud*, Transl. James Strachey, Vol. XXI, Vintage Classics, London, 2001.

Sigmund Freud, "Fragments of an Analysis of a Case of Hysteria", in *The Complete Psychological Works of Sigmund Freud*, Transl. James Strachey, Vol. VII, Vintage Classics, New York, 2001, p. 28.

Sigmund Freud, "Project for a Scientific Psychology", in *The Standard Edition of the Complete Psychological Works of Sigmund Freud*, Transl. James Strachey, Vol. I, Vintage Classics, London, 2001.

Sigmund Freud, Joseph Breuer, "On the Psychical Mechanism of Hysterical Phenomena: Preliminary Communication from Studies on Hysteria", in *The Standard Edition of the Complete Psychological Works of Sigmund Freud*, Transl. James Strachey, Vol. II, Vintage Classics, London, 2001.

Timothy Gantz, *Early Greek Myth: A Guide to Literary and Artistic Sources*, John Hopkins University Press, Baltimore, 1993.

Frédéric Gros, *Disobey! A Philosophy of Resistance*, Transl. David Fernbach, Verso Books, 2020.

Hugo Grotius, *On the Law on War and Peace: Three Books*, 1625.

Camille Kouchner, *The Familia Grande, A Memoir*, Transl. Adriana Hunter, Other Press, 2022.

Immanuel Kant, *Groundwork of the Metaphysics of Morals*, Transl. Mary Gregor, Cambridge University Press, 1996.

Jacques Lacan, *The Seminar of Jacques Lacan, Book VII. The Ethics of Psychoanalysis*, Ed. J.-A. Miller, Transl. Dennis Porter, W.W. Norton & Co., New York/London, 1992.

Jacques Lacan, *The Seminar of Jacques Lacan. Book X*, "Anxiety", Ed. J.-A. Miller, Transl. A. R. Price, Cambridge, Polity, 2014.

Jacques Lacan, *The Seminar of Jacques Lacan. Book XII, The Object of Psychoanalysis*, December 1965. Unpublished.

Jacques Lacan, *The Seminar of Jacques Lacan. Book XX, Encore*, Ed. J.-A. Miller, Transl. Bruce Fink, W.W. Norton & Co., New York/London, 1999.

Jacques Lacan, "Presentation on Psychic Causality", in *Écrits. The First Complete Edition in English*, Transl. Bruce Fink, W.W. Norton & Co., London/New York, 2006.

Jacques Lacan, "Psychoanalysis and Its Teaching", in *Écrits. The First Complete Edition in English*, Transl. Bruce Fink, W.W. Norton & Co., London/New York, 2006.

Jacques Lacan, "Kant with Sade", in *Écrits. The First Complete Edition in English*, Transl. Bruce Fink, W.W. Norton & Co., London/New York, 2006.

Jacques Lacan, "Radiophonie", in *Autres Écrits*, Seuil, Paris, 2001.

Jacques Lacan, *Television: A Challenge to the Psychoanalytic Establishment*, Transl. Denis Hollier, Rosalind Krauss, and Annette Michelson, Ed. J. Copjec, W.W. Norton & Co., New York, 1990.

Philippe Lançon, *Disturbance, Surviving Charle Hebdo [Le Lambeau]*, Transl. Steven Randall, Europa Éditions, 2019.

Laurent, Éric, "Comments on Three Encounters Between Feminism and the Sexual Non-Relation, *Psychoanalysis Lacan*, 5, Online Journal of Lacan Circle Australia, trans. Mia Lalanne, available online: https://lacancircle.com.au/psychoanalysislacan-journal/psychoanalysislacan-volume-5/comments-on-three-encounters-between-feminism-and-the-sexual-non-relation/

Clotilde Leguil, *Les Amoureuses, voyage au bout de la féminité*, Seuil, Paris, 2009.

Simon Liberati, *Eva*, Le Livre de poche, Paris, 2016.

Jacques-Alain Miller, "L'Un tout seul" [The One All-Alone], *L'Orientation lacanienne*, Teaching pronounced at the Department of Psychoanalysis of the University of Paris 8, Course of 25 May 2011. Unpublished.

George Orwell, *Nineteen Eighty-Four*, Modern Classics, 2013.

Ovid, *Metamorphoses*, Transl. David Raeburn, Penguin Classics, 2004.

Marcel Proust, *The Captive, Vol 5 of In Search of Lost Time*, Transl. C.K. Scott Moncrieff, Chatto & Windus, 2017.

Marcel Proust, *Albertine Gone, Vol 6 of In Search of Lost Time*, Transl. Terence Kilmartin, Chatto & Windus. First English Edition, 1989.

Pascal Quignard, *L'Homme aux trois lettres*, Grasset, Paris, 2020.

François Regnault, "Laissez-les grandir!", *La Cause du désir*, 2020, n° 105.

Alain Rey, *Dictionnaire historique de la langue française*, Le Robert, Paris, 2000, p. 410.

Jean-Jacques Rousseau, *The Social Contract or Principles of Political Right*, Transl. G.D.H. Cole, public domain.

Vanessa Springora, *Consent: A Memoir*, Transl. Natasha Lehrer, Harper Collins, 2021.

Virginia Woolf, *A Woman's College from the Outside*, Book Classic, 1926.

Filmography

Gaslight by George Cukor, 1944.
Vertigo by Alfred Hitchcock, 1958.
Contempt by Jean-Luc Godard, 1963.
Deer Hunter by Michael Cimino, 1978.
Full Metal Jacket by David Lynch, 2001.

Index

For Product Safety Concerns and Information please contact our EU
representative GPSR@taylorandfrancis.com
Taylor & Francis Verlag GmbH, Kaufingerstraße 24, 80331 München, Germany

www.ingramcontent.com/pod-product-compliance
Lightning Source LLC
Chambersburg PA
CBHW070351270326
41926CB00017B/4084